Fascinating Facts
A Dictionary of Amazing Information

Fact is stranger than fiction, as this book will show you. Open a page at random and you will be amused, amazed, stunned and enthralled by the information you will find there.

Did you know, for example, that a caterpillar has over 2000 muscles in its body; that Milan Cathedral took 579 years to build; that the diameter of the earth's orbit is almost exactly 1000 times the distance that light travels in one second, or that a kangaroo can only jump when its tail is on the ground?

If you want to be the mastermind of your family, class or gang you will find *Fascinating Facts* an invaluable aid. It contains more interesting information than you dreamed existed!

Gyles Brandreth needs no introduction as the author of many popular books, and in addition *Fascinating Facts* is illustrated with cartoons by David Mostyn.

The Chip Book of
FASCINATING
FACTS

compiled by

Gyles Brandreth

illustrated by David Mostyn

A Hippo Book
Scholastic Publications Limited
London

Scholastic Publications, Ltd.
161 Fulham Road, London, England

Scholastic Magazines, Inc.
50 West 44th Street, New York, NY, USA

Scholastic Tab, Richmond Hill,
Toronto, Ontario, Canada

Ashton Scholastic, Gosford,
New South Wales, Australia

Ashton Scholastic, Penrose,
Auckland, New Zealand

First published by Scholastic Publications, Ltd., 1980
Text copyright © Gyles Brandreth 1980
Illustrations copyright © David Mostyn, 1980
All rights reserved

Made and printed in Great Britain by
Hazell Watson & Viney Ltd
Aylesbury, Bucks
Set in Baskerville

ISBN 0 590 70004 9

Introduction

When I was at school we played a game called the Word Game. The rules were simple. One of the players would think of a word – any everyday word would do – and call it out. The other players would then race to see which of them would be the first to come up with a fascinating piece of information that had something to do with the given word. For example, if somebody called out the word EGG and you knew that it takes forty minutes to boil an ostrich egg, you'd be the winner.

Although I loved playing the Word Game, I wasn't the winner very often. I was no mastermind: I simply didn't know enough. Of course, if I had owned a copy of this book when I was playing the Word Game I would have won every time. It's an extraordinary A to Z of everyday words with a fascinating fact for each of them. Now you too can play the Word Game. All you have to do is think of a word, look it up and be amazed.

This *Dictionary of Amazing Information* may not be the biggest dictionary in the world – look up the word DICTIONARY on page 35 and find out what is! – but it is certainly the only one of its kind. It's packed with remarkable information: some of it useful, some of it useless, most of it unusual and all of it *true*.

A
There is a city in Sweden called A.

abbey
Westminster Abbey was built at a time when the congregation numbered about sixty people.

abdomen
American strong man Frank Richards could withstand the pounding of a sledge-hammer against his abdomen. However, he surpassed even this feat when he developed the technique of withstanding the force of 47·2kg (104lb) cannon ball fired at his abdomen from close range.

abolish
The army of Costa Rica, in Central America, was abolished in 1948 because the president said the people loved peace and an army was no longer necessary.

abracadabra
Abracadabra is a magic word used by many magicians. Originally an abracadabra was a charm to cure hay fever.

accent
Accents were first written in the French language in the early 17th century.

accident
The use of ether as an anaesthetic was discovered by accident, by an American chemistry student who had seen the effect of the gas on young people who sniffed it at parties for fun.

acre
There are over three times as many acres in the three counties of North Yorkshire, South Yorkshire and West Yorkshire as words in the Bible.

addition
The opposite sides of a cubed dice always add up to seven.

address
Postal addresses with numbers for houses began in Paris in 1463.

albinos

Albinos are distinctive because unlike most people they have white hair and pink eyes. However, in the Book of Enoch, which was probably written one hundred years before the birth of Christ, Noah is described as an albino. According to the Bible story, when he grew up Noah not only built the Ark and saved the animals but he also repopulated the earth with men. Since albinism is transmitted from one generation to the next, it is surprising that there are not more albinos among us!

alcohol

A society campaigning against alcohol in Northern Australia was forced to disband through lack of support.

A

ale
Ale was often drunk at breakfast in England, up until the nineteenth century.

allergy
John Churchill, the first Duke of Marlborough, was allergic to cabbage.

alphabet
The twenty-six letters in our alphabet can be rearranged 620,448,401,733,239,439,369,000 different ways.

altar
Altars were not used by the early Christians. They were introduced to churches from pagan worship.

altitude
In the autumn of 1978 a West German climber reached the top of Mt. Everest 8848m (29,028ft) having climbed all the way without artificial oxygen, the highest altitude man can climb in the world.

ambulance
Ambulances were developed by Napoleon's surgeon and were first used to carry the wounded during the Italian campaign in 1796–7.

America
America is named after an Italian explorer, who first found the American mainland in 1499. His name was Amerigo Vespucci.

ammunition
Cannon balls were used in royal naval guns until 1837 when they were replaced by shells.

amputation
Dominique Larrey, the personal surgeon to Napoleon Bonaparte, could amputate a leg in fourteen seconds.

anaconda
The anaconda is the longest and heaviest snake living. Fully grown anacondas can measure 10·6m (35ft) long and they can weigh as much as 113·4kg (250lb).

anaesthetics
Anaesthetic drugs were used by the French army as early as 1812. At first they were only used 'locally', to numb a limb or an injured part of the body, which relieved the pain but left the wounded patient conscious. The first 'general' anaesthetic, under which the patient became fully unconscious, was not given until 1848.

anagrams
Anagrams are words or phrases formed by the rearrangement of the letters of other words or phrases. They are a marvellous way of showing off your intelligence. Here are a few popular ones: 'Christianity'='I cry that I sin'; 'elegant'='neat leg'; 'Old England'='Golden Land' and 'punishment'='nine thumps'.

animals
Aristotle believed that animals could be produced out of decaying meat and mud.

ant
An ant is capable of lifting fifty times its own weight.

Antarctica
The coldest place in the world is in Antarctica. The average temperature there is −57·8°C (−72°F).

anti-freeze
It was made illegal to sell anti-freeze to the Indians in Quebec, Canada.

antlers
A deer's antlers are usually shed each year and are replaced by larger ones.

apple
The French novelist Alexandre Dumas was once instructed by his doctor to eat an apple every morning underneath the Arc de Triomphe at 7am. He hoped it would help him to sleep better.

apricot
The oil from apricots is used in cosmetics, sweets and food flavouring.

A

aqueduct
Water is still brought to the town of Segovia in Spain in an aqueduct built by the Romans in 110 BC.

Arabic
There is no single word in Arabic for a 'camel'.

archery
A statute issued during the reign of Henry VIII made it illegal for full-grown men to practise archery over a distance of less than 240yds (219·5m).

archaeologist
An Italian archaeologist, Giovanni Belzoni, had difficulty making a living from archaeology and used to support himself by being a professional strong man. His star turn was to carry eleven men around the stage while they were sitting on an iron frame.

area
The total surface area of the earth is estimated to be 510,066,100sq km (196,937,600sq miles).

arid
The most arid place on earth is probably the Desierto de Atacama in Chile. Until 1973 no rain had fallen there for 400 years.

armadillo
The nine-banded armadillo is very precise about its babies. The mother always gives birth to four young, either four male or four female, but they are never mixed.

armistice
The armistice at the end of World War I was signed at the eleventh hour of the eleventh day of the eleventh month of 1918.

armour
William the Conqueror could jump onto a saddled horse wearing full armour.

arms
Thomas Topham who lived in England in the eighteenth century could snap his fingers while a man danced on each of his outstretched arms.

army
Cyrus the Great, King of Persia in the sixth century BC, knew the names of all the men in his army of four thousand troops.

arrest
When the notorious Edwardian murderer Dr. Crippen left England on a trans-Atlantic voyage to North America, he thought he had escaped arrest by the English police. However, the ship on which he was sailing was fitted with the recently invented wireless telegraphy equipment. The English authorities sent a wireless signal to the ship and Dr. Crippen became the first person to be arrested by means of radio signals.

arrow
In 1798 Sultan Selim of Turkey shot an arrow 889m (972yds), over half a mile.

ash
The European ash grows at an average rate of 30·5cm (12in) a year, during its first hundred years.

Asia
The continent of Asia, not including Europe, covers almost one-third of the land surface of the earth.

aspirin
Aspirin is prepared from a chemical called Salicylic Acid. This chemical is found in the roots, leaves, blossoms and fruit of several different trees and plants, in particular the group called 'spirea', which are shrubs that belong to the Rose family. These are found throughout the Northern Hemisphere and are frequently used in decorations and bridal wreaths.

astronaut
Aleksei Leonov became the first astronaut to walk in space on March 18, 1965. The first astronaut to step onto the moon was Neil Armstrong on July 21, 1969.

A

astronomer
The Greek astronomer Hipparchus, who lived in the second century BC, measured the size of the moon, made the first accurate star map and devised a method for calculating the positions of planets in the universe.

athletics
The ancient Olympic Games which were established in the thirteenth century BC were abolished in 393 AD, and athletics disappeared from Europe for about 1,400 years before being revived in the early nineteenth century.

atlas
A national atlas of Britain appeared in 1579.

atmosphere
The pressure in the sea increases by one atmosphere for every thirty feet of descent.

atom
The first atomic bomb was exploded on July 16, 1945.

attack
In the battle of Passchendaele in 1917 the British forces lauched eight attacks over 102 days and gained 8km (5miles).

auction
At an auction in Liverpool in 1890 the auctioneer used a mummified cat as a hammer.

audition
Over 1,400 actresses auditioned for the part of Scarlett O'Hara in the film of *Gone with the Wind*. The part was given to Vivien Leigh.

authoress
Enid Blyton wrote a total of 600 children's stories during her career. In 1955 she was completing them at the rate of one in just over six days.

autobiography
The first autobiography in English was written by an Elizabethan composer called Thomas Whyteham in 1576.

autograph
Julius Caesar's autograph has been valued by experts at over £1,000,000.

Azores
The Azores, islands in the Atlantic, are in fact the peaks of submarine mountains, part of a 16,093km (10,000 miles) long range, which runs along the ocean floor. It is called the Atlantic Ridge.

B
The shape of the letter B is very like the Egyptian hieroglyphic (symbol) for a house.

babies
Four babies are born every second.

backbone
The largest living animal without a backbone is the giant squid.

badger
The badger is the largest meat eating mammal living wild in the British Isles.

badminton
Badminton probably developed from an old children's game called 'battledore and shuttlecock'. Its modern name comes from Badminton Hall in the west of England where it became very popular at about 1870.

B

bagpipes
The Scots are not the only people to play the bagpipes.
The ancient Greeks used to play an early type which they
called a 'symphoneia'.

balloon
The first successful balloon was designed by Etienne
Montgolfier and launched in 1783.

bamboo
Bamboo is not a tree; it is really a wood grass.

banana
The banana is the largest known plant without a solid
trunk. In fact botanically the banana is a herb.

bank
The first English bank was founded by Francis Child in
1603.

banquet
A large mummy frequently attended banquets held by
priests in ancient Egypt. It was a constant reminder that
death was never far away.

barber
As part of a publicity drive in 1909 a London barber,
Robert Hardie, was blindfolded and then shaved a
customer in twenty-seven seconds.

bat
The bat is the only flying mammal.

bath
Queen Elizabeth I used to have a bath once a month.
This was considered as extraordinary cleanliness by her
courtiers.

batting
The great Australian batsman, Sir Donald Bradman,
had a batting average of 99·94 runs in fifty-two test
matches, spanning twenty years.

battle
The last British monarch to fight in battle was George II,
at the battle of Dettingen in 1743.

bayonet
The bayonet was first made in Bayonne, France.

beans
Baked beans were originally served with molasses. The idea of adding tomato sauce instead did not catch on until fifty years after they were first eaten.

bear
Bears are so strong that they have been known to break the neck of fully grown bison with one blow.

beast of burden
Donkeys and horses were the first animals tamed by man to act as beasts of burden, over 7,000 years ago.

beaver
A beaver's teeth never stop growing.

bed
Louis XIV had 413 beds.

bees
Each year more people die from bee stings than from snake bites.

beech
During the First World War the German soldiers were encouraged to smoke beech leaves instead of tobacco. This idea was not very successful.

B

beer
In Tibet and parts of Nepal the people drink a type of beer made from rice. They call it 'chang'.

beetles
Beetles outnumber any other living creature on earth. There are 3,700 species found in Britain alone.

belch
Belching is considered to be a compliment on good food in many eastern countries.

bells
Henry VIII once lost the bells of St. Paul's Church, after losing at gambling.

Bible
Apparently the word 'and' is used in the Bible 46,227 times, whereas 'reverend' and 'girl' only appear once. If you have nothing else to do on a rainy day, why not count them?

bicycle
Alphonse Duhamel built a clock out of old bicycle parts.

Big Ben
Even if you are ten miles away from Big Ben you can still hear the hour being struck.

bill
The Duke of Marlborough used a tavern bill on which to write the first news of his victory at the battle of Blenheim in 1704.

billiards
Mary Queen of Scots was a skilful billiards player.

billion
In Britain a billion is one million million (1,000,000,000,000) but in the USA it is only one thousand million (1,000,000,000).

bingo
There are roughly 44,000,000 ways of making bingo, on a bingo card with ninety-nine numbers.

bison
A prehistoric bison was discovered in the frozen ground of central Alaska in 1938 with most of its hair and skin still intact.

black beetle
This is a common name for a cockroach. It is not very accurate, however, because a cockroach is brown and it is not a beetle.

blackberry
Blackberries can be used to make wine, hair dye, a medicine for curing whooping cough and a delicious refreshing drink for people running a high temperature.

Black Death
During the Black Death in Europe, in the fourteenth century, one person in four died from the plague.

bleeding
Because doctors used to believe that bleeding helped the sick, Louis XIII of France was once bled forty-seven times in one month!

blotting paper
Blotting paper was discovered by mistake. A careless worker forgot to add the substance which should have made the paper smooth and it ended up with a hairy surface on which the ink could not flow. However, someone realized the use of this new paper and the mistake was allowed to continue.

boa-constrictor
A boa-constrictor called 'Popeye' lived to be forty years old, the greatest age ever recorded for a snake.

boat
The fastest speed a boat has reached is 527·8kph (328 mph). It was called *Blue Bird* and was driven by Donald Campbell in 1967.

bone
Babies are born with about 350 bones. Some of these later join together and therefore adults end up with 206 bones, normally.

B

books
During his lifetime George III bought over 67,000 books, including 200 Bibles.

boots
George IV (1763–1830) was the first person to wear a pair of boots which had been made to fit each of his feet. Until that time all boots and shoes could be worn on either foot.

booty
When Sir Francis Drake returned from his voyage of 1580 he brought back booty which even in those days was worth £600,000.

bottle
The largest champagne bottle is called a Nebuchadnezzar. It can hold 16 litres (28·14pt) of wine.

bow
In Winnipeg, Canada it is forbidden to use a bow and arrow in the street.

bowler
Jeff Thompson, the Australian fast bowler, can bowl a cricket ball at 160kph (100 mph).

bowls
Archaeologists believe that a form of bowls was played in ancient Egypt in the sixth century BC. Men were bowling at targets in England by the thirteenth century AD.

boxing
The longest recorded boxing match lasted for 7 hours 19 minutes and included 110 rounds. The fight ended without a verdict because both boxers were unable to continue.

brake
Brakes on all four wheels of a car did not become a standard feature until the 1920s. Some manufacturers who had fitted brakes to all four wheels of early models even removed them on later ones in the early days of motoring.

brain
The human brain is 80 percent water.

bread
In Turkey it is considered extremely unlucky to step on a piece of bread lying on the ground.

breathing
We normally breathe sixteen to eighteen times a minute and in twenty-four hours we breathe in about 11·32cu m (400cu ft) of air.

breech-loading
The first breech-loading gun was invented in 1751, yet it was 130 years before the principle was adopted by the Admiralty for naval guns.

brickmakers
The Coomas are a caste of brickmakers in India who have also practised plastic surgery since the fifth century AD.

bricks
Bricks are the oldest man-made construction material still in existence. They were used in Egypt 7000 years ago.

bride
In many Indian weddings the husband does not see his bride until their wedding day.

B

bridge
The card game we call 'bridge' originated in Turkey.

bright
The brightest star that we can see is Sirius, the Dog Star.
The light that reaches us from Sirius takes over eight and
a half years to travel through space and astronomers have
calculated that Sirius is twenty-three times brighter than
our own Sun.

bubblegum
All bubblegum contains some rubber. Rubber is the
substance that makes blowing the bubble possible.

buckle
Until the invention of the shoe-string (or shoelace) in
1790 shoes had been fastened with buckles.

Buddha
Buddha means 'the enlightened one'.

building
The tallest inhabited building in the world is the Sears
Tower in Chicago, USA. It is 443m (1,454ft) high. The
tallest self-supporting structure in the world is the CN
tower in Toronto, Canada. This has an elevated restaurant 347·5m (1,140ft) above the ground.

bulls
Contrary to popular belief, bulls cannot distinguish red
from any other colour. Matadors who used white capes
in the bull-ring, instead of the traditional red capes,
found that the bulls reacted in exactly the same way,
despite the colour change.

burial
Ben Jonson had to be buried in a sitting position because
the plot allocated to him in poet's corner, in Westminster
Abbey, was not big enough for normal burial.

burrow
Ants and termites can burrow to a depth of 24·3m (80ft)
to find water.

butcher
The eighteenth century name for a butcher was a 'flesh-flogger'.

buttercup
There are 1,200 species of buttercup.

butterfly
Butterflies do not taste with tongues, they use their back feet instead.

buttons
Buttons were probably worn as decorations first. Their practical use was realized sometime later.

buzzing
There is an anti-noise law in the Canadian capital, Ottawa, which bans the buzzing of bees.

C

C is an abbreviation for Centigrade and for Conservative. C is also the Roman numeral for 100, and the name of the key-note in the 'natural' major scale in music.

cabbage
Cabbage consists of 91 per cent water.

cake
A cake 16·45m (18yds) long, 7·31m (8yds) wide and 0·45m (1·5ft) thick was presented by Frederick William I of Prussia to his army of 30,000 men, in 1730. Because of its size the cake had to be drawn to the feast by eight horses.

calculating machine
Blaise Pascal invented a calculating machine when he was nineteen years old.

calculus
Sir Isaac Newton was only twenty-four when he devised the method of calculation now called 'calculus'.

C

calendar
When the Gregorian calendar was adopted in Britain in 1752, eleven days had to be dropped from the existing calendar in order to correct it. This led to rioting because many people felt that part of their lives had been taken away.

calories
We use eight times as many calories walking fast as we use writing a letter.

camel
It is against the law to use camels on the roads of British Columbia, Canada.

canal
There are 35·4km (22 miles) more of canal in Birmingham than in Venice.

canned food
A can of veal taken on an expedition to the Arctic in 1824 carried these opening instructions: 'Cut round on the top with chisel and hammer'. The can was made of iron.

cannon
Sergeant Hawthorne, a British army instructor in the early twentieth century, used to be able to support a 181·5kg (400lb) cannon on his shoulder while it was fired and hold it there against the recoil.

canyon
The Grand Canyon, Arizona, is 349km (217 miles) long and up to 2,133m (7,000ft) deep in places.

car
The first all-British car was the 1895 Lanchester.

cards
Paul von Boeckmann of New York could tear a hole in a pack of cards by using just his thumb and forefinger.

carp
In certain parts of Germany people eat carp on New Year's Eve to bring good luck in the coming year.

carpet
The oldest carpet so far discovered has an average of 2,700 knots to every 6·45sq cm (1sq in).

carrot
Carrots are made into a form of porridge in India, a wine in Britain and are used as a substitute for coffee in Germany.

cartoon
The first coloured cartoon in a newspaper appeared in the *New York World* in 1895. It was called 'The Yellow Kid'.

cats
Cats can draw their claws into sheaths in their paws.

caterpillar
A caterpillar has over 2,000 muscles.

cathedral
Milan cathedral took 579 years to build and can seat a congregation of 40,000 people. It is the second largest cathedral in Italy and the second largest church in Italy, after St. Peter's Basilica, in Rome.

Catholics
There are more Roman Catholics in the world than all other Christians added together.

caviar
Caviar is thirty percent protein.

cells
Red blood cells live about 127 days. About 8,000 are destroyed and replaced every hour.

centigrade
The centigrade thermometer was invented by a Swedish astronomer called Andreus Celsius.

centre
The centre of the earth is almost 6,440km (4,000 miles) beneath our feet.

cereal
The first breakfast cereal was Shredded Wheat. It was produced in Colorado in 1893.

ceremony
The coronation ceremony for British monarchs has remained virtually unchanged since Whit Sunday 973, when Edgar was crowned king at Bath, by St. Dunstan.

chair
During his thirty-five year reign, in the late sixteenth century, the Holy Roman Emperor Rudolf II presented a steel chair to the city of Augsburg, in Germany. The chair had taken thirty years to make and cost £20,500.

champagne
Frederick the Great of Prussia used to drink coffee made with champagne instead of water.

Channel Islands
The Channel Islands were the only part of the United Kingdom occupied by Germany during the Second World War.

characters
There are over 500 characters in the great Russian novel *War and Peace* by Leo Tolstoy.

cheese
There is a market at Hoorn in the Netherlands which sells nothing but cheese.

cheetah
The cheetah is the fastest running land mammal. It can reach speeds of up to 100kph (62·1mph) over short distances.

cheques
The first English banker's cheques were printed in 1760.

chess
There are more than 170,000,000,000,000,000,000,000,000,000 different ways of playing the ten opening moves in a game of chess.

chestnut
Conkers from horse chestnuts are used for feeding cattle and horses in the eastern counties of England. Pigs will not touch them though.

chew
The nineteenth century politician and Liberal prime minister W. E. Gladstone always chewed each mouthful of food thirty-two times before swallowing.

chimney
The oldest account of a chimney describes one in Venice in 1347.

China
The Chinese name for China is 'zhong kuo'. It means 'the middle kingdom'.

chocolate
The Spaniards were the first people to eat chocolate in Europe; it had been imported from Mexico in 1520. The first chocolate factory was opened in Berlin in 1756.

christian names
A nineteenth century French composer, Louis Julien, was actually christened with all the christian names of his thirty-six god-parents!

Christmas cards
Twenty per cent of the Christmas cards sold today are sold in aid of charities.

Christmas Day

There were seven British sovereigns living on Christmas Day in 1683 and 1684. Try and work out who they were.

Christmas tree

The practice of erecting fir trees inside houses as part of the special celebrations associated with Christmas is quite a recent idea. Although there is some evidence to suggest that Christmas trees were in use in Alsace in the last twenty years of the sixteenth century, the first written account of one dates from 1605 and it describes a fir tree decorated with paper in a house in Strasbourg (eastern France). Lighted Christmas trees are not recorded before 1660 when the first mention of trees decorated with candles was made.

chronometer

Chronometers are easier to check and keep accurate with modern instruments and communications than they were in the eighteenth century. Even so the chronometer which Captain Cook took on his voyage in 1772 was only 7 minutes 45 seconds slow after three years at sea.

churches

There are as many churches as days of the year in the city of Colula in Mexico.

cicada

The female cicada can hear her mate calling 1·6km (1 mile) away.

cider

Cider in the west of England is called 'scrumpy'. Some scrumpy is so potent that in many pubs strangers are only allowed to drink it in half-pints.

cigar

The cigar gets its name from the Mayan word for smoking 'sik'ar'.

city

The oldest city in the world is Damascus, the capital of Syria.

clam
Clams have been recorded living in the sand for 100 years.

clock
I'Hsiang and Liang Lin-tsan made the first mechanical clock in China in AD 725.

clover
A clover-shaped coin was minted in England in 1060. By breaking off the four leaves the owner could use them as separate coins.

club
The earliest known club was a dining club in London established in 1413, the year Henry V became king.

coal
The coal mined in Britain was formed 270,000,000–300,000,000 years ago.

cobweb
Spiders never spin cobwebs on chestnut wood.

cockroach
Even with its head cut off a cockroach can live for several weeks.

Coca-Cola
By the end of 1976 over 185,000,000 bottles of Coca-Cola were being bought each day throughout the world.

cod
A cod weighs about 5,000 times more than its brain.

coins
Peter the Great of Russia could snap silver coins with his fingers.

cold
'Acute Nasopharyngitis' is the scientific name for the common cold.

Colosseum
Sea battles used to be fought in the Colosseum in Rome. The arena was flooded and armed ships fought against each other.

C

colour-blindness
People who suffer from colour-blindness most frequently have trouble with the colour green.

combs
The ancient Syrians were making combs in about 1000 BC.

comedy
The earliest English comedy was written by the headmaster of Eton and was performed by his pupils in 1553.

comet
Halley's comet takes seventy-six years to travel once round the sun. It will next reappear in 1986.

comic
The earliest British comic was called *Ally Sloper's Half Holiday* and it first appeared in 1884.

concerts
The first concerts in the world at which the audiences had to pay for their seats were given by the English violinist John Bannister in London in 1672.

concrete
Concrete was used by the Romans in their construction industry. The first concrete roads in Britain were built in 1865.

conquer
It took the forces of the Ottoman empire twenty-five years to defeat the Venetians and conquer the island of Crete in the middle of the seventeenth century.

continent
The first and last letters are the same in the names of four out of five continents (Africa, Australia, America, Asia).

copper
There is more copper in the brain and liver of a baby than those of an adult.

cork

The ancient Greeks used cork to split marble. Dried cork was forced into cracks in the rock, it was then soaked with water which caused it to expand and split the rock.

corkscrew

When Maurice, Count of Saxony, was on a picnic and found that the corkscrew had been left behind, he bent a nail into the right shape with his fingers and used that to open the wine bottles.

cosmetics

Poppea, the wife of the Roman emperor Nero, used to make herself a cosmetic face-mask from bread crumbs and asses milk which she wore all night.

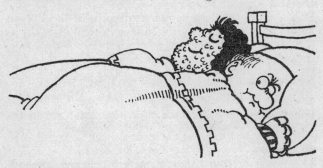

cream

Cream is lighter than milk.

creation

Dr. Lightfoot, a seventeenth century vice-chancellor of Cambridge university, claimed that the earth and man-kind had been created by 9.00 am on October 23, 4004 BC.

cremation

Half the people who die in Britain today are cremated.

cricket

A cricket can jump one hundred times its own length, which is the equivalent of a man jumping about 183m (200yds).

D

crosswords
Crosswords in the *Daily Telegraph* shortly before the allied invasion of Normandy in 1944 included many of the top-secret code names, quite by coincidence.

crown
The crown used in the coronation of British monarchs weighs nearly 2·26kg (5lb).

crystals
Snow crystals are hexagonal.

D

D is used by modern printers to represent the Roman numeral for 500. However, 500 was written originally as half of the Tuscan numeral ⓪ or CIↃ.

daffodil
Another name for the daffodil is the Lent lily.

dam
Four of the ten highest dams in the world are in the USSR.

dandelion
The leaves of young dandelions are delicious in sandwiches or as an addition to salads.

darts
Darts is the most popular sporting activity in Britain. At least one person in ten plays darts.

dates
There are over 35,000,000 date palms in Iraq, which supply more than 80 per cent of the world's dates.

Dead Sea
There is so much salt in the Dead Sea that it is almost impossible to drown in it.

deaf
Ludwig van Beethoven was completely deaf when he composed his Ninth symphony.

death
In the early days of death certificates many doctors experienced difficulty explaining the causes of death. Here is one written in the USA in the nineteenth century 'Went to bed feeling well but woke up dead.'

debt
At the end of the seventeenth century the national debt in Britain was under £5.20 per person. Today it is over £1,400 per person.

decay
According to dentists we are most likely to suffer from tooth decay if we eat fudge or plain chocolate. If we have to eat sweet things, doughnuts are the least harmful to our teeth.

decree
During the sixteenth and seventeenth centuries it was decreed that anyone found drinking coffee in Turkey would be put to death.

deer
The roe deer is probably the fastest native mammal in Britain. It can run up to 65kph (40mph) for short periods.

defeat
In 1757 an Anglo-Indian army, commanded by Robert Clive, defeated an Indian army twenty times its size at the battle of Plassey.

defence
There were only fifty men serving in the whole of the US Air Force at the beginning of World War I in 1914.

delay
There was a delay of fifty-six years between the conception of photography and the practical application of that theory.

delta
The delta caused by the two great Indian rivers the Ganges and the Brahmaputra covers an area of 75,000sq km (30,000sq m).

D

density
The earth is 5·517 times more dense than water.

dental drill
We should have no fear of the modern dental drill, powered by high-speed machinery, when we remember that the first dentist's drill was only driven by a spinning wheel which could vary in speed as the dentist worked, or even stop altogether.

dentists
Early dentists in Japan often used to extract teeth by pulling them out with their fingers. They used to practise special exercises which strengthened their finger grip.

dentures
An English aristocrat called Lord Hervey ordered a set of ornamental dentures in 1735. They were made from Italian agate and had to be removed before he could eat anything. George Washington's were made of ivory, and tasted so horrible he soaked them in port each night.

depth
The Marianas Trench in the Pacific Ocean is 11·03km (6·85 miles) deep. An object dropped into the sea over this deep depression would take an hour or more to sink to the bottom.

descendant
Robert the Bruce, hero king of Scotland who defeated the English at the battle of Bannockburn in 1314, was in fact the descendant of a French aristocrat.

desert
The Sahara desert covers an area as large as Europe. In fact it is larger than the combined area of the next nine largest deserts in the world.

dialect
There are at least eight principal dialects of Chinese which are so different from each other that the speakers of one cannot understand any of the others. However, they all use the same system of writing.

diameter
The diameter of the earth's orbit is almost exactly 1000 times the distance that light travels in one second.

diamond
The most valuable diamonds are coloured blue-white.

dice
The ancient Greeks used to make their dice from the ankles bones and shoulder blades of sheep.

dictionary
The *Oxford English Dictionary* is the largest English dictionary in the world. When it was compiled each usage of a word was written on a slip of paper. After twenty-two years' work the editors were faced with a pile of paper weighing 1·75 tonnes.

differential
The differential gearing system used to drive many cars today was known to the ancient Chinese before the birth of Christ.

dinner
The Duke of Queensbury, an eighteenth century aristocrat, used to eat five full-course dinners each evening between 5.00pm and 3.00am.

disc
A disc of stone, which showed signs of having been worked into shape, fell from the sky near Tarbes, in France, in 1852.

discovery
Christopher Columbus discovered America by mistake. He was really looking for China and the East Indies.

divorce
In Morocco a husband can divorce his wife by repeating 'I divorce thee' three times.

D

doctor
Ancient Chinese doctors had to hang a lantern outside their houses for every one of their patients who died. Too many lanterns did nothing to improve the doctor's business!

dodo
The dodo was a strange looking bird which belonged to the pigeon family and lived on the island of Madagascar. Because it was prized as a source of food by European sailors it was hunted to extinction in 1680.

dog
A four-year-old dog which fell over a cliff and dropped 91m (300ft) to its base, picked itself up and scampered off. Its only injuries were two bloodshot eyes.

dolphin
Despite its name the killer whale is classified as a dolphin.

double-bass
A double-bass constructed in 1849 was so large that it had to be fitted with foot levers to assist the musician playing it.

downhill
In 1976 Tom Simons of the USA reached a speed of 194·5kph (120·8mph) skiing downhill in Italy.

dragon-fly
During an experiment a dragon-fly ate forty house-flies in less than two hours.

drain
The Cloaca Maxima, one of the great drains of Rome, was built in 588 BC and is still in existence. In England the first public officials responsible for drains were not appointed until 1513.

dress
Catherine de Medici, Queen of France, possessed a dress which at present day prices would cost £6,000,000. She wore it only once.

drink

The Revised Statutes of Manitoba, Canada make it illegal for anyone to drink beer in 'a privy, lavatory or toilet'.

driving

The Prince of Wales, later King Edward VII, was the first member of the British royal family to drive a car. He bought his first car in 1899.

E

duck
A mallard duck flying over a golf-course was hit by a ball driven by golfer Jim Tollen. The bird was killed instantly and fell onto a green named after a nearby pub – the pub was called 'The Mallard'.

duelling
In eight years at the beginning of the seventeenth century two thousand French aristocrats died fighting duels.

dune
The sand dunes at Arcachon in France are 106·6m (350ft) high.

E
E is the most frequently used letter in the English language.

earnings
In 1685 the average earnings of a peasant in England were four shillings (20p) a week.

earring
Pirates believed that piercing their ears and wearing earrings improved their eyesight.

earth
The earth is approximately 4,600,000,000 years old. Its equatorial circumference is 67·14km (41·72 miles) greater than its polar circumference. The earth travels more than 2,400,000,000km (1,500,000,000 miles) each day.

earthquake
In April 1884 there was an earthquake in East Anglia which killed four people.

eating
A fifteenth century Scottish clan is reputed to have killed and eaten over 1,000 people in twenty-five years.

eclipse
During a total eclipse the sun's corona comes into view but because of the speed at which the sun moves a solar eclipse can never last longer than 7 minutes 58 seconds.

eels
In 1918, sand-eels fell from the sky near Sunderland for ten minutes.

egg
An ostrich egg has the same volume as two dozen hen's eggs. It takes forty minutes to boil, one-and-a-half hours to hard boil and a man weighing 127 kg (20 stone) can stand on the shell without it cracking.

electricity
Angélique Cottin, a fourteen-year-old French girl, was one of the earliest cases of scientifically examined 'electric people'. She could knock over heavy pieces of furniture with a gentle touch and people touching her suffered what appeared to be violent electric shocks.

elements
Chemists arrange the basic chemical elements into what is called the Periodic Table of Elements, which helps to classify the similarities among groups of elements. This 'Periodic Law' was first devised by a Russian chemist called Dmitri Ivanovich Mendeleyev, who followed the discovery of the relationship of elements with similar atomic weights, made by earlier nineteenth century chemists, and devised his own generalization that: 'the elements arranged according to the magnitude of atomic weights show a periodic change of properties'.

elephant
The first elephants were not much bigger than modern pigs. Elephants living today have 0·45 kg (1 lb) of brain for every 453 kg (1000 lb) of body weight, and the African elephant, which always sleeps standing up, is on its feet for fifty years.

embalming
After Sir Walter Raleigh's execution in 1618 his wife had his head embalmed and carried it everywhere with her until her own death twenty-nine years later.

emperor
The Emperor Napoleon, who had conquered Italy by the time he was twenty-six, was terrified of cats.

E

emu
An emu can run at 48kph (30mph).

encyclopaedia
Early in the fifteenth century Chinese scholars began to compile a huge encyclopaedia called the *Yung Lo Ta Tien*. When it was finished it consisted of 11,095 volumes, but because it was too large to print it had to be copied twice by hand. All three copies have been lost.

energy
The earth only receives 1/2,000,000,000 of the Sun's energy sent into the universe.

engineer
Isambard Kingdom Brunel was one of the greatest engineers of the nineteenth century. He constructed bridges and railways, built the first trans-Atlantic paddle-steamer, the *Great Western*, in 1837, the first iron-hulled screw-driven steamer, the *Great Britain*, in 1843, and in 1858 he launched the prototype of the modern ocean liner, the double-iron-hulled *Great Eastern*.

English Channel
David Morgan of Scarborough swam across the English Channel when he was only thirteen.

epic
The biblical epic *Quo Vadis* was filmed three times. On the last occasion in 1951, the director Mervyn Le Roy employed 30,000 extras and sixty-three lions.

epilepsy
Alexander the Great and Caius Julius Caesar were two of the greatest generals in history. They were also epileptics.

epistle
The Third Epistle of St. John is the shortest book in the Bible.

epitaph
A suitable epitaph for one Dr. Fuller read 'Here lies Fuller's Earth.'

equals sign (=)
The equals sign (=) was first used in an algebra text written in 1557.

equator
Eratosthenes calculated the circumference of the equator over 2,000 years ago – he was only 383km (238 miles) out. As the earth whirls round on its axis a spot on the equator moves at over 1,600kph (1,000mph).

ergatocracy
Try using this word if you want to make an impression on other people. 'Ergatocracy' is another word for 'workers'.

escalator
In 1898 the first escalator in Britain was installed in the famous London shop called Harrods. When it was first used attendants were positioned at the top to offer brandy or smelling salts to anyone overcome by the experience of travelling on the moving staircase.

E

escape

Apart from the amazing feats of escape that he performed, Harry Houdini specialized in exposing fraudulent seances.

Eskimos

Eskimos use refrigerators to stop their food from freezing.

estuary

The estuary of the river Ob in the USSR is 725km (450 miles) long.

Eucharist

Lord Strathallen was one of the highland chieftains who was mortally wounded at the battle of Culloden in 1746. Before he died he had to take the Holy Eucharist, but because neither bread nor water were available on the battlefield, whisky and oat cake were used.

eureka

'Eureka' shouted Archimedes when he jumped out of his bath after making his famous discovery about specific gravity. Sitting in the bath thinking over a scientific problem he suddenly realized that a body immersed in fluid is supported by the force equal to the weight of the displaced fluid: when Archimedes sat down in his bath the water level rose. When the early settlers founded the state of California they gave it the word 'Eureka' as a motto, because of the gold which had been discovered there.

evacuation

In 1940, 338,226 French and British troops were evacuated from the beaches at Dunkirk in north-east France.

evaporation

7,500,000 tonnes of water evaporate from the Dead Sea every day.

execution

Scanderburg, a fifteenth century king of Albania, once executed two prisoners, who were bound together, by cutting them in half at the waist with one blow of his sword.

exhibition
An exhibition of German sausages held in Bern in 1909 produced no less than 1,785 varieties of sausage.

export
In 1975 a company based in Cambridge exported 1,800 tons of sand to the desert state of Abu Dhabi in the Persian Gulf.

express
The Osaka–Okayama Express, in Japan, averages 166·2 kph (103·2 mph).

extinction
There are many animals and birds in the world which are threatened with extinction. Some of the most critical cases are the Javan Rhinoceros with an estimated eighty survivors, the Whooping Crane with fewer than sixty survivors and the Japanese Crested Ibis of which there are less than ten.

eye
The starfish has an eye on the end of each arm.

eyebrows
In Renaissance Italy it was the fashion to shave off one's eyebrows.

F
F is used as an abbreviation in a variety of different cases. F means 'fine' when describing a pencil-lead; it is the initial for the Fahrenheit temperature scale, and it refers to a 'fellow' of a society or college.

face
After Queen Elizabeth I lost her front teeth, she was concerned that her face had sunk inwards. So whenever she appeared in public she used to stuff her mouth with cloth to fill it out.

falls
More people die of falls than from any other kind of household accident.

F

family
In theory the offspring of a pair of Norway rats could grow to a family of 350,000,000 in only three years.

famine
During the Irish potato famine in the middle of the nineteenth century an estimated 1,500,000 people died.

fashion
During the Middle Ages it was the fashion among court ladies in France to wear corsets on top of their other clothes, not underneath as modern ladies do.

fast
When the crew of Apollo X re-entered the earth's atmosphere in 1969 they were travelling at 39,897kph (24,790·8mph), faster than any man had travelled before.

fat

There is enough fat in the human body to make seven bars of soap.

feat

Among the most daring feats performed by the French tightrope walker, Charles Blondin, was a back somersault on stilts. This is difficult enough when you are on the ground – but Blondin was 51·8m (170ft) above the ground with no safety net beneath his tightrope.

February

February is named after a Roman festival of purification.

feed

The giant blue whale, the largest living animal, feeds on plankton, tiny animals and plants which cannot be seen with the naked eye.

felt

Some of the earliest clothes worn by man were made from animals hairs beaten into felt.

fence

There is a wire fence in Queensland, Australia which is 1·8m (6ft) high and stretches for 5,531km (3,437 miles).

fertilizers

One of the more unusual fertilizers used in England was a shipment of 180,000 mummified cats which had been found in an ancient grave in Egypt. It was sent to Liverpool in 1890.

fiction

Most fiction written in Elizabethan England was meant to be read aloud.

fiddle

Contrary to popular belief the Emperor Nero did not play his fiddle while Rome burnt in 64 AD. The instrument was not invented until the thirteenth century.

fifteen

The first time a rugby team was fielded with fifteen players was in 1875. Until then any number of people had played on both sides during a match.

F

filling station
There are filling stations beside roads in almost every town and village today which makes it difficult to believe that the first road-side petrol pump appeared less than sixty years ago, in 1920. It was installed near Newbury in Berkshire.

films
Hollywood film companies were producing an average of two films a day in 1939.

film star
The first film star to appear on a postage stamp was Grace Kelly, now Princess Grace of Monaco. A special stamp was issued to commemorate her marriage to Prince Rainier in 1956.

fine
In the province of Saskatchewan in Canada you can be fined for drinking water in a beer parlour.

finger
Anne Boleyn, the second wife of Henry VIII, had an extra finger on her left hand.

fire
Only six people died in the Great Fire of London in 1666.

fish
There are at least 20,000 species of fish.

fist
South African strong-man, Oom Cornelius Joubert, had a quick temper. Once, when he was angry with a horse, he gave it one blow with his fist and the animal dropped down dead.

flag
The national flag of Denmark, a white cross on a red background, was introduced in 1219. It is the oldest national flag in the world.

flag-pole
There is a flag-pole 67m (220ft) high at the US Merchant Marine Academy in King's Point, New York, USA.

flame
Flames that shoot out from the sun can be thousands of kilometres/miles high. The biggest recorded so far was 1,689,765km (1,050,000 miles) high.

flatfish
A type of flatfish called the sand dab is so thin that light can shine through it.

flight
The first sustained controlled flight by a powered aircraft was made by Orville and Wilbur Wright on December 17, 1903.

floating
If you add sugar to a glass of water and then put an egg into the water, the egg will float.

flogging
Flogging was abolished in the British army and navy in 1881.

flowers
Over half of all the known types of flowers in the world grow in South Africa.

foam rubber
The first foam rubber was made by beating latex in a food mixer.

food
A dragon-fly traps its food by forming its legs into a basket.

football
A form of football called 'Tsu Chu' was played in China at about 350 BC. Football has been played in England from the twelfth century, but no rules were created until 1846.

fountain
The fountain at Fountain Hills, Arizona, USA has a column of water 170m (560ft) tall, when it is running at full pressure. The weight of all this water is estimated to be eight tonnes.

G

frogs
In 1882 living frogs enclosed in lumps of ice dropped out
of the sky over Iowa, USA.

fuel consumption
With the change to the metric system, the increased cost
of petrol, and the greater number of people driving in
foreign countries, calculating fuel consumption and converting mpg to kml is becoming increasingly important.
A simple way of converting the figures is to remember
that: 1 mpg=0·354km1 and 1km1=2·825mpg.

G
When the pronunciation of C and K became identical in
Latin there was a need for an additional letter to represent
the second sound, and a new symbol G was introduced
to replace the sound of the lost C. It first appeared around
234 BC, according to surviving inscriptions.

galaxy
The world's largest telescope can pick out about
1,000,000,000 galaxies in the universe. They are all
rushing away from each other, some at speeds of
112,650kph (70,000mph). In our own galaxy there are
about 100,000,000,000 stars, and the sun is situated about
32,000 light years from its centre.

gale warnings
The earliest gale warnings were issued in 1861.

galley
War galleys rowed by prisoners were still in use during
the reign of Louis XIV of France, in the 17th century.

gallon
The Imperial gallon was created by an Act of Parliament
in 1824. One gallon of pure water weighs 10lb (4·53kg).

gate-posts
Today people erect stone balls on top of their gate-posts
where in the past it was customary to stick the heads of
enemies or criminals. In Northern Ireland many gate-
posts have pointed tops which stop the fairies or lepre-
chauns from sitting on them.

gauge
There are different gauges of railway track in use in the world. In the UK there are three in use. The widest gauge in the world is used in the Indian sub-continent and in Argentina and Chile. They use a gauge of 1·676m (5ft 6in) wide. At the other end of the scale are the narrow gauge railways between Ravenglass and Eskdale in Cumbria and the Romney, Hythe & Dymchurch line in Kent, which are only 0·381m (1ft 3in) wide.

genius
Thomas Young, who later became a famous eighteenth century physicist and Egyptologist, was able to speak twelve languages by the time he was eight years old.

geyser
There are twenty geysers on the Kamchatka peninsular in the USSR.

ghosts
There are reported to be more ghosts per square mile in Great Britain than in any other country.

glacier
For over one hundred years climbers on the Begbic glacier in western Canada have seen the body of a man perfectly preserved in the slow moving ice. The body will not become accessible for burial until 1982.

gland
There may be as many as 3,000 sweat glands to every 6·45sq cm (1sq in) of skin on the palms of our hands.

glass
A ball made of glass will bounce higher than a rubber ball.

glider
Gliders have climbed to an altitude of 12,894m (42,302ft) and flown at a speed of 175kph (108mph).

glow-worm
The most efficient form of light production so far discovered is the glow-worm.

G

glutton
An American trencherman called Bozo Miller ate 250 ravioli in 1 hour 10 minutes.

God
The word for God in the Basque language, of south-west Europe, is 'Jingo'.

gold
Nearly two-thirds of the world's gold is mined in South Africa.

golden disc
Glen Miller's *Chattanooga Choo Choo* was the first song to be awarded a golden disc for selling over 1,000,000 copies.

golf
Tommy Moore, a young American golfer, scored a hole-in-one when he was only six-years-old.

golliwog
The original golliwog was auctioned in 1917 and then donated to the Prime Minister, David Lloyd-George. It now lives at the Prime Minister's country house Chequers, in Buckinghamshire.

goodnight
'Goodnight' was the last word spoken by Lord Byron, the nineteenth century romantic poet.

goose
An extraordinary coincidence happened to Noel McCabe of Derby when he was listening to a record called *Cry of the Wild Geese* – one Canadian Goose crashed through his window and two others fell into the garden outside.

gorilla
A gorilla has no hair on its chest, although it has hair almost everywhere else on its body.

Gondwanaland

190,000,000 years ago the earth was divided into two vast continents which we now call Gondwanaland and Eurasia.

governor

Before becoming lieutenant-governor of Jamaica in 1672, Sir Henry Morgan had been a pirate.

gown

Queen Elizabeth I owned 3,000 gowns.

gramophone

Mary had a little lamb was the entire contents of the first gramophone record, which was made in 1877.

grave

Early men used to dig their graves with the shoulder-blades of prehistoric mammals.

gravity

The gravity on the surface of the white dwarf companion of the star Sirius is 250,000 times greater than the gravity on the earth's surface.

grenade

Alfred Blazis, an American soldier during World War II, could throw a grenade 86·7m (284ft 6in).

greyhound

Greyhounds have the best eyesight of all dogs.

guinea pig

The first people to make use of guinea pigs were the Incas. They not only kept them as pets, but also used them as a source of food, and as sacrifices to their gods.

gums

Many women in the eighteenth century had their gums pierced with hooks in order to keep their dentures in place.

gun

A gun with 144 barrels was invented in 1387. Its rapid firing made it an ancestor of the machine gun.

H

gunfire
It was a common belief that gunfire produced rain. In 1910, a group of British farmers tried to postpone a naval gunnery exercise because the expected rain would damage their crops.

gut
Catgut comes from sheep.

gymnastics
In the 1976 Olympic Games, Nadia Comaneci of Rumania was awarded seven perfect scores. She was only fourteen years old at the time.

H
The Romans used H to represent 2·5. The Roman 2 was II and a dash (–) across cut it in half giving H=2·5.

haggis
The ancient Greeks used to eat haggis over 2,000 years ago. They called it 'koila prodateia.'

hail
246 people were killed by hailstones in Moradabad, in India, in 1888.

hair
William Shakespeare, Henry VIII, and Oliver Cromwell all had red hair. As a rule red-haired people have fewer hairs than dark-haired and fair-haired people, but no matter what colour our hair it all grows at about the same rate, 0·43mm (0·01714ins) in twenty-four hours.

haircut
Howard Hughes, the eccentric American millionaire, insisted that his barber used three dozen new combs and new scissors every time he cut his hair.

half-mast
The first time a flag was flown at half-mast as a mark of respect for the dead was in 1612. It was lowered to that position on board a ship called the *Heartsease* after the captain had been killed by Eskimos.

hamster
Hamsters live for ten years, which is three years longer than a gerbil, but three years less than a guinea pig.

hand
An Austrian named Johann Hurlinger walked from Vienna to Paris on his hands in fifty-five days. His average speed for the 1,400km (871 mile) journey was slightly over 2·5kph (1·5mph).

handkerchief
In 1785, King Louis XVI of France issued a law which decreed that handkerchiefs had to be square.

hanging
A cow was publicly hanged in France in 1740 after being found guilty of sorcery.

hangover
Dr. Pemberton invented Pepsi Cola in 1886 as a cure for hangovers.

hare
Running flat out a hare can reach a speed of 72·41kph (45mph).

hawk
A young hawk is called an eyas.

Hay Fever
Hay Fever was one of the most popular comedies written by the English playwright Noel Coward. He must have felt that it was going to be a success because he wrote it in three days from start to finish.

hazel
The hazel tree was regarded as being so sacred in Ireland that anyone who felled one was put to death. It still has special powers even today – diviners use hazel twigs to find water underground.

head
Many ancient Roman statues were made with detachable heads to save work. One head could simply be replaced by another.

H

headmaster
In 1859, Henry Montagu Butler was made headmaster of Harrow School. He was only twenty-six years old.

head-on
A head-on collision between two cars occurred in Redruth, Cornwall in 1906, which may not seem very unusual except that they were the only cars in the town at that time.

healing
King Edward I is claimed to have cured 1,736 sick people in 1300 by just touching them with his hand.

hearing aid
An enormous hearing aid was made for King John VI of Portugal in 1819. The device was actually a throne in which the king sat. Servants spoke into openings in the hollow arms and their voices passed into a pipe at the back which the king held against his ear.

heart
A man's heart weighs about 326gm (11·5oz) but a woman's only weighs about 241gm (8·5oz). The human heart beats about 100,000 times in twenty-four hours and in that time it pumps a total of 8,182 litres (1,800 gallons) of blood.

heating
The most famous library in the ancient world, which was built at Alexandria in Egypt, was destroyed by the Saracens in 604 AD. All the books were used as fuel to heat the public baths; according to some historians the supply lasted six months!

height
A flea can jump over 100 times its own height.

helicopter
Leonardo da Vinci made a model of a helicopter in the fifteenth century.

Hell
Hell is not only the place of punishment after death; it is also the name of a railway station in Norway.

herd
Everyone knows that a group of cattle are called a herd, but did you know that a group of foxes is called a 'leash', a group of horses is called a 'harras', and when you see a collection of goats you should refer to them as a 'trip'.

herring
Throughout the world more herrings are eaten than any other type of fish, perhaps because herrings have the same nutritional value as steak.

high heels
King Louis XIV of France was the first person to wear high-heeled shoes, in the seventeenth century.

high tide
High tides around the world are usually 12 hours 25 minutes apart. In the Bay of Fundy on the northeast coast of USA high tides sometimes rise over 14m (47ft).

hijack
The first aerial hijack took place in 1948. A group of Chinese bandits seized control of a flying-boat travelling between Macao and Hong Kong, in the Far East.

hippopotamus
Although a hippopotamus weighs nearly 3,629kg (8,000lb) and has a stomach over 3m (10ft) long, it can still run faster than a man.

history
The nineteenth-century historian Charles Kingsley resigned from his post as Professor of Modern History at Cambridge University because, as he said, 'history is largely a lie'.

honey
The ancient Egyptians used to preserve their dead in large jars of honey. When archaeologists tasted some of this honey centuries later they found that it was still edible.

I

horse
The modern horse developed from an animal which was no bigger than a modern fox. It was called a Hyracotherium.

horseshoe
Apart from being one of the world's most famous painters and designers, Leonardo da Vinci was also a man of unusual strength – he could break a horseshoe with his bare hands.

hospital
In the eighteenth century the second Earl of Montague opened a hospital for old cows and horses.

House of Lords
When Prince Charles became Duke of Cornwall at the age of three, he also became eligible to sit in the House of Lords.

hovercraft
The hovercraft was developed by Sir Christopher Cockerell in 1955. Today test hovercrafts have reached a speed of 378kph (234·8mph).

humming-birds
Humming-birds are the only birds that can fly backwards.

hymn
The rousing hymn 'Onward Christian Soldiers' was written by Sir Arthur Sullivan, who is, perhaps, better known for the light operas he wrote with W. S. Gilbert.

hypnotist
A Hungarian hypnotist called Laslo Biro invented the first successful ball-point pen. When the first throw away biros appeared in British shops in 1959, 53,000,000 were sold in the first year, almost one biro for every person in the country.

I
'I' is the most commonly used word in English conversation.

ice
In 1887 thousands of sheep in Texas were killed during a violent ice storm.

iceberg
The average iceberg weighs 20,000,000 tons.

ice-breaker
The largest ice-breakers can clear a passage through ice 2·1m (7ft) thick.

ice-cream
In 1790 George Washington spent $200 on ice-cream in two months.

identical
In the Bible the nineteenth chapter of the second book of Kings and the thirty-seventh chapter of the book of Isaiah are identical.

igloo
A census taken among Eskimos in the 1920s indicated that fewer than 1 in 46 had ever seen an igloo.

ignition key
Ignition keys were first used to start cars in 1949.

illegal
A law passed during the reign of Charles II made it illegal to bury the dead in anything but woollen garments.

immigration
Britain had nearly 180,000 immigrants in 1976.

import
It seems surprising, but camels have to be imported into the vast desert kingdom of Saudi Arabia.

inch
In the beginning an inch was reckoned to be the width of a thumb, but in the fourteenth century Edward II decreed that an inch should be the length of three barleycorns (grains of barley) laid end to end.

India
India has one-quarter of all the cattle in the world.

I

Indian clubs
In 1913 a boxing instructor called Tom Burrows swung a pair of Indian clubs for 107 hours. During that time he swung each club 770,000 times.

indoors
The first recorded ascent in a hot air balloon took place indoors at the Casa da India, Portugal in 1709.

industry
The oldest industry in New York is the fur trade which began in 1615.

infantry
More Roman infantry were killed in the one-day battle of Cannae in 216 BC than the total number of men killed in the Royal Air Force in both world wars.

infinity (∞)
The infinity sign was introduced into science by John Wallis in 1655.

inflation
Inflation was so severe during the American War of Independence (1775–78) that in America the price of wheat rose 14,000 per cent and the price of beef 33,000 per cent.

influenza
More than a 1,000,000 people in Europe died of influenza during the epidemic which followed the end of World War I. The total number of deaths throughout the world was 20,000,000.

ingredients
It is perhaps wiser not to ask what are the ingredients of haggis, but experts expect these to be included: the liver, heart and lungs of a sheep, oatmeal, onions, suet and a boiled bag made from the sheep's stomach.

inherit
Henry III inherited the throne when he was eight months old.

inn
The last inn on the Faroe Islands closed in 1918.

insects
There are approximately 21,500 species of insect in Britain.

insomnia
Catherine the Great, Winston Churchill and Napoleon Bonaparte all suffered from insomnia.

instruments
Harps and flutes were being played in Egypt about 6,000 years ago and drums may well have been played before then.

insurance
When life insurance first became available many speculators took out policies on the lives of well-known people. Highwaymen, soldiers and others involved in risky occupations were the most popular.

I

interview
When Prince Philip appeared on the BBC programme 'Panorama' in 1961 he was the first member of the British royal family to be interviewed on television.

intestine
The large intestine is 1·21–1·52m (4–5ft) long and the small intestine is three to four times as long as a person is tall.

invasion
During the Allied invasion of Sicily in 1943 181,000 men were landed in three days.

inventor
One of the most creative inventors in history was Leonardo da Vinci. Amongst his many inventions perhaps the most notable were screw propellers, sluice-gates, swimming-belts and scissors.

invisible
A fourth century BC Greek philosopher, Democritus, was the first person to suggest that matter consisted of tiny invisible particles.

iron
In 1908, a mass of iron estimated to weigh 40,000 tonnes fell out of the sky over Siberia.

island
Apart from Australia, which is geographically regarded as a continent, Greenland is the largest island in the world.

Italian
Italian is really Tuscan, the language of Tuscany.

ivory
Until this century much of the world's ivory came from the tusks of prehistoric mammoths which had been found in north-eastern Siberia.

ivy
Ivy is the only evergreen climber in Britain.

J

All the letters of the alphabet except J are contained in the twenty-first verse of the seventh chapter of the book of Ezra, in the Old Testament.

jack

A 'jack' is the name given to a pike when it is still a small fish.

jackdaw

The jackdaw gets its name from the sound is makes, 'chack'.

jade

The ancient Chinese believed that jade had the power of endowing immortality. In the second century BC Prince Liu Sheng had two funeral suits made for himself and his wife, each one consisting of over 2,000 squares of jade.

jaguar

The jaguar catches fish with its paws.

jam

Friday, February 13, 1976 was a particularly unlucky day to be driving in Oxford Street, London – there was a jam of fifty-two buses, one behind the other.

January

January is named after Janus, the Roman god of doorways. He is depicted with two faces, one looking forwards the other looking backwards, so that he could watch over the 'entrance' to the new year.

Japan

The Imperial family of Japan have ruled in an unbroken line of descent for over 2,000 years. Emperor Hirohito is the one-hundred-and-twenty-fourth successor of the first emperor Jimmu Tenno.

Jaws

The film *Jaws* made an average of £5,000,000 a week during its first two-and-a-half months' showing in America.

J

jazz
The Jazz Singer was the name of the first full length talking film, made in 1927.

jeep
Nearly 649,000 jeeps were manufactured during World War Two. At peak production they were being produced at the rate of one every eighty seconds.

jellyfish
The jellyfish called the 'Portuguese Man-of-War' is not one single animal but a whole colony of small ones.

Jericho
The great walls of Jericho were destroyed by an earthquake. In the Bible they collapsed after a great shout was sent up by the besieging army.

Jerusalem artichoke
The vegetable we call a Jerusalem artichoke has nothing to do with Jerusalem and is not an artichoke. It is a member of the same plant family as the common sunflower and it was first cultivated in Italy.

Jesus
In Hebrew the word 'jesus' means 'a saviour'.

jet
The fastest jet in the world flies at almost 3,530kph (2,194mph).

jewels
There are over 400 jewels in the St. Edward's Crown which is used to crown British monarchs.

jigsaw puzzle
The famous 'Festival of Britain' jigsaw has over 40,000 pieces.

jockey
Frank Wooton, the English champion jockey 1909–1912, rode his first winner when he was only nine years old.

John O'Groats

There was a real man called John O'Groats who lived on Duncansby Head, the northernmost point of Scotland, during the sixteenth century.

journey

The train journey across the USSR from Moscow to Vladivostock is 9,600km (6,000 miles) long and takes nine days.

judge

Following the rebellion led by the Duke of Monmouth in 1685 Judge Jeffries sentenced 330 people in the west of England to be hanged, and 841 to be transported overseas for ten years or more.

judo

Judo developed from the ancient Japanese martial art 'ju-jitsu'.

juggernaut

We call huge lorries 'juggernauts', but originally 'juggernaut' was the title given to the Hindu god Krishna. An enormous idol of this god was dragged through the streets once a year and the more devout worshippers used to throw themselves under the trailer which carried it.

juggling

Paul Spaddoni is the only man ever to juggle six raw eggs at one time.

Jumbo

During three-and-a-half years' work in the circus, Jumbo the elephant gave rides to an estimated 1,000,000 children.

jump

A kangaroo can only jump when its tail is on the ground.

juvenile court

One of the defendants brought before the first session of the first juvenile court was charged with shouting 'celery' in the street.

K
In physics K stands for the Kelvin which is the unit of thermodynamic temperature.

kaleidoscope
The first kaleidoscope was made in 1816.

kangaroo
The first time explorers in Australia saw this animal they asked a native aborigine what it was. However, because he did not understand their question the aborigine replied 'kan-ga-roo', which meant 'I don't know' in his own language.

kayak
In 1928, E. Romer of Germany crossed the Atlantic in a kayak. He had to remain sitting for all fifty-eight days of the voyage.

kettle-drum
The kettle-drum had been in use for 700 years before a method of tuning it was discovered in 1837.

kidneys
The heart pumps about 1·27 litres (2·25pts) of blood through our kidneys every minute and the kidneys filter as much as 28·41 litres (50 gals) of fluid every day.

kilt
Kilts originated in France before they were worn in Scotland.

king
Jean I of France was king for only four days.

King Kong
In the original film of *King Kong* the monster was actually played by a hand puppet 15·24cm (6in) high.

kipper
In Anglo-Saxon a 'kipper' was a young salmon, in the nineteenth century it meant a dried and cured cod and today when we talk about a 'kipper' we mean a dried and cured herring.

kiss
Two American actors, Regis Toomey and Jane Wyman, held a kiss for over three minutes in the 1941 film *You're In The Army Now*.

kitchen
A kitchen set up to deal with a serious famine in India served 1,200,000 meals a day in April 1973.

kite
The design of the first aeroplanes was modelled on the shape of box kites.

kiwi
The kiwi lays the largest egg of any bird in proportion to its size. It is not uncommon to find hen kiwis which have laid eggs that weigh more than one-quarter of their own body-weight.

knitting machine
William Lee invented a knitting machine in 1589.

L

knot
The collective term for toads is a 'knot'. So the next time you see a group of toads you will know to call them a 'knot' and not anything else!

kung fu
Translated literally the Chinese words 'kung fu' mean 'leisure time'.

L
The Roman numeral for fifty was written L. In America L is an abbreviation for an elevated railway.

ladybird
There are forty-five small beetles that are classified as ladybirds. One of them has the scientific name *Subcoccinella vigintiquatuorpunctata*!

lagoon
The Lagoa dos Patos in Brazil covers an area of 10,645sq km (4,110sq miles).

languages
In India there are 845 different languages.

larch
The European larch is one of the fastest growing conifers. By the age of fifteen the tree grows at the rate of 1m (3·28ft) a year.

larva
The larva of the polyphemus moth eats 86,000 times its own weight.

lawyers
Half the men who signed the American Declaration of Independence and two-thirds of the men who became presidents of the USA were lawyers.

leg
Centipedes have one pair of legs attached to every segment of their bodies.

legal code
Ur-Nanmu is a code of laws that was drawn up in the ancient city of Ur in 2145 BC.

lemon
Alfred Moss was a staff sergeant in the British army renowned for his skill with a sword. He could cut the thread holding a lemon above the ground and then slice the fruit twice before it hit the floor.

lemon juice
During the Indian Mutiny the British sent secret messages written with a mixture of lemon juice and milk.

lens
17,000 lenses have been counted on the eye of a butterfly.

leopard
After killing its prey a leopard will lift it up into a tree to stop other meat-eating animals from stealing its food.

letters
There are seventy-two letters in the Cambodian alphabet.

library
The United States Library of Congress houses over 73,000,000 items on 563km (350 miles) of shelves.

Libya
The official initials for Libya are SPLAJ. They stand for the Socialist People's Libyan Arab Jamahiriya.

life
The Russian monk, Rasputin, who seemed to possess mystical powers during his life, was very reluctant to die. His assassins were forced to drown him in the end, after he had continued to live despite eating enough poisoned cakes to kill an army!

lifeboat
The first lifeboat was designed by a landsman who had never lived by the sea and who had no personal experience of sea wrecks.

lift
Some passenger lifts operate at 33kph (20mph).

light
The only time when the number of hours of light equals the number of hours of dark is at the two equinoxes in March and September.

lightning

When lightning struck a cowshed in 1901, it killed the first cow nearest the door, missed the second, killed the third one and continued this pattern. Out of the twenty cows in the shed the ten odd numbered ones were killed but the ten even ones were not even scorched.

lightning conductor

Benjamin Franklin invented the lightning conductor on the basis of an experiment he made in 1752. He flew a kite during a violent thunderstorm when the string carried a charge down to a key he had tied to it. The spark that jumped from the key proved that lightning is an electrical phenomenon. The next two men to try this experiment were both killed by lightning.

light year

One light year is the distance travelled by light in a year, roughly 9,462,000,000,000km (5,880,000,000,000 miles). This means that the light which reaches us today from Alderbaran, sixty-eight light years away, left that star in 1911.

line

The railway line that runs from Moscow to Nakhodka in Siberia is 9,334km (5,799 miles) long.

ling

The ling is a fish related to the cod. It lays about 28,000,000 eggs at one time of which fewer than 1,000,000 hatch and live.

lips

Crown Prince William of Germany once permitted Annie Oakley, the legendary markswoman, to shoot the ash from a cigarette he was holding between his lips. She was firing from a distance of 30m (100ft).

liquid

On average we drink about 1·5 litres (2·5pts) of liquid every twenty-four hours.

livestock

Between 1710 and 1795 the weight of livestock reared in Britain more than doubled.

L

living
On earth the living are outnumbered by the dead by approximately thirty-to-one.

lizard
The brain of the thirty-five tonne prehistoric lizard the Brontosaurus weighed 45g (1lb).

loch
Loch Morar in Scotland is 310m (1,617ft) deep.

lock gate
The swinging lock gate was invented by Leonardo da Vinci. In 1487 he built six of them for the Duke of Milan.

locomotive
When George Stephenson's locomotive 'Locomotion' pulled the first train along the Stockton to Darlington line in 1825, it reached 24kph (15mph). In 1938 another steam locomotive 'Mallard' reached a speed of 202kph (126mph) and the British Rail High Speed Train travels at a speed of 201kph (125mph), though it has reached 228·8kph (143mph) in early runs.

long-bow
The usual range for the long-bow was 274–457m (300–500yds). However, Robin Hood could shoot an arrow almost twice that distance.

longitude
The meridian (line of longitude) 170°W reaches from the North pole to the South pole without hitting any land except for a few Pacific islands, and Antarctica.

long-jump
When Bob Beaman (USA) established a new World long-jump record at the 1968 Olympics, he beat the record that had previously existed by a staggering 0·55m (1ft 9½in).

London
Until 1957, London was the largest city in the world.

low
The surface of the Dead Sea is the lowest depression in the world. It is 395m (1,296ft) below sea level.

lunar eclipse
There can only be a lunar eclipse when the moon is full and there are never more than three lunar eclipses in one year; in fact in some years there are none at all.

lung
The left lung holds less air than the right.

lung-fish
The lung-fish can live on land for three years.

M
M is used in aerodynamics to represent the mach number, the ratio of the speed of a body to the local speed of sound. Mach 2 is twice the speed of sound.

Magna Carta
King John did not sign Magna Carta in 1215. The king could not write. He stamped the famous document with his royal seal instead.

magnet
There is a giant magnet near Moscow which weighs 36,000 tonnes and has a diameter of 60m (196ft).

mammal
Mammals range in size from the blue whale, which can be 33·58m (110ft) long to the pigmy shrew which is no bigger than a man's thumb.

map
A map of the river Euphrates flowing through Mesopotamia was made over 5,000 years ago.

margarine
Margarine gets its name from the Greek word for a pearl.

mashed potato
Instant mashed potato was made by the early natives of Peru. They left potatoes on the ground to be frozen and then broke them up to grind them into a powder. By adding water to the powder later they could make mashed potato.

M

matches
There is enough phosphorus in the human body to make the heads of 2,000 matches.

mathematics
Lord Kelvin, a leading nineteenth century scientist, mathematically proved that flying in a heavier-than-air machine is impossible.

may bug
The Polish name for a may bug seems impossible to pronounce. It is 'chrzaszcz'.

meat
The people of Uruguay eat more meat per person than any other nation in the world. On average they consume 309g (11oz) per day.

medieval
The average medieval man was only 1·67m (5ft 6in) tall and weighed about 61kg (9st 6lb).

merchant ship
The first atomic merchant ship was called the *Savannah* and she was launched in 1959.

message
A message in a bottle dropped by an American ship in 1941 floated 2,011km (1,250 miles) across the Pacific in only fifty-three days. Unfortunately the native who found it could not read any of the eight languages in which it was written.

meteors
About 1,000,000 meteors reach our atmosphere every hour but five times as many can be seen after midnight as can be seen before.

metre
French scientists in 1791 devised the metre from their calculations of the length of one quarter of a circle round the earth. One metre is one ten-millionth of that length.

Mickey Mouse
Mickey Mouse only has four fingers.

microscope
Zacharius Jansen invented a microscope in about 1590.

midget
A thirty-two-year-old midget who acted as a spy during the French Revolution used to be carried through the enemy lines disguised as a baby.

migration
Measurements taken on Golden Plovers during migration have shown that they have flown 3,862km (2,400 miles) in twenty-four hours and have lost only 907g (2lb) in weight. They must be one of the most economical consumers of energy in existence.

mildew
The Romans used to worship a god of mildew. His name was Robigus.

mile
'Mile' takes its name from two Latin words *mille passuum*, which mean '1,000 paces'. This was the Roman measure of distance. It was 142 yards (129m) shorter than an English statute mile, making it 493m (1,618yds).

M

milk
Throughout the world goat's milk is used more widely than milk from cows.

Milky Way
The Milky Way contains at least 1,000,000,000 stars and the distance from one side to the other is about 100,000 light years, or 100,000 times 9·65 million million km (100,000 times 6,000,000,000,000,000 miles).

mill
A nineteenth century Scotsman invented a miniature mill for twisting twine which was powered by a mouse.

mine
Until the middle of the nineteenth century naval mines, used during wartime, were called 'torpedoes' even though they floated in the same place and never moved.

minerals
The sea is rich in minerals. In every 4·16 cu km (1 cu mile) of sea water there are 4,000,000 tonnes of magnesium and the oceans contain 99 percent of the world's bromin.

mint
At one time there were seventy mints making coins in England alone, which is more than all the mints in the whole world today.

mirage
Several explorers in Alaska claim to have seen a mirage of the city of Bristol, in the west of England, hovering on the Alaskan skyline. There is even a local tradition in Alaska that the city can be seen every year for twenty days in June and July.

model
William Fuqua, an American male model, could stand perfectly still for four-and-a-half hours. He made a lot of money from literally doing nothing.

mole

Although moles are only about 15.24cm (6in) long they are very strong. In a night a mole can dig a tunnel over 91m (100yds) long and one mole was found swimming in a Scottish loch 2.41km (1.5 miles) from the shore.

Mongols

In the thirteenth century the Mongols conquered all of northern Asia and China, and yet their total population was no greater than that of one of the large Chinese cities at the time, about 1,000,000 people.

monk

The first champagne was invented by a blind Benedictine monk, Dom Pierre Pérignon, at the turn of the sixteenth century. There is a famous champagne named after him, Dom Pérignon.

monkey

As they grow older male monkeys lose the hair on their heads just as adult humans lose theirs.

monopoly

The amount of Monopoly money issued each year, dollar for dollar, exceeds the total printed by the US treasury.

monster

'Nessiterasrhombopteryx' is one of the suggested scientific names for the Loch Ness monster.

month

Every month each red blood cell travels round the human body 43,000 times.

moon

Measurements suggest that the surface of the moon is made of many layers of fragile rock. After the crew of Apollo 12 landed on the moon the surface continued to vibrate for nearly an hour.

morals

A society was formed in Belgium in 1877 to improve the morals of domestic cats.

M

mosquito
Male mosquitoes do not bite, so you can blame the female ones next time.

mother
In a great majority of the world's languages the word for 'mother' begins with an 'm' sound.

motion
The Greek scientist Ptolemy believed that the earth was stationary in the universe and never moved.

motorist
In 1888 the Sultan of Turkey became the first member of any royal family to drive a car.

motto
The German motto of the Prince of Wales, *Ich Dien* ('I serve'), was taken by the Black Prince from John, King of Bohemia after his death at the battle of Crécy in 1346. The prince also adopted the dead king's crest of three ostrich feathers.

mountains
Thirteen of the world's twenty highest mountains are in the Himalayas, the other seven are in the nearby Kara-korum range. If all twenty were laid end to end they would almost reach from London to Gloucester 163km (101 miles).

mourning
Until the Middle Ages mourners in England wore white. White is still the colour of mourning in China and most Moslem countries, but in Turkey the colour is neither black nor white but violet.

mouth
One quart of saliva is produced in the mouth each day, equal to slightly more than one litre.

multiplication

Multiplication, far from being boring, can be a source of endless fun. Take 142857 for example. Multiply it by 1, 2, 3, 4, 5, or 6 and you will always end up with the same figures in the same order but starting from a different point: $142857 \times 5 = 714285$, $142857 \times 2 = 285714$. Multiplied by 7 and you get a row of 9s, multiplied by 8 you get 1142856, add the first 1 to the last number and you end up with $1 + 142856 = 142857$. Even when multiplied by numbers over 100 this pattern still appears: $142857 \times 258 = 36857106$, add 36 to the last number $857106 + 36 = 857142$. Try it, but watch out for multiples of 7, they produce rows of 9s if you use the same method of addition.

murder

Buhram, a member of the violent Indian cult of Thugee, murdered over 900 people in fifty years by strangling them.

muscles

There are 600 muscles in our muscular system, and we use seventeen of them to smile and forty-three to frown.

museum

Oxford boasts the oldest museum in the world. It is called the Ashmolean Museum.

N

N is an abbreviation for North and for the scientific unit of force the Newton, named after the seventeenth century mathematician Sir Isaac Newton.

nail

There is enough iron in the human body to make a nail.

name

Middle names were once illegal in England.

napkin

Giles Rose, one of Charles II's favourite chefs, wrote a book in 1682 giving instructions for folding table napkins into twenty-six different shapes.

naval battle
The battle of Salamis, fought off the coast of Greece in 480 BC, involved about 190,000 men fighting in an estimated 1,110 ships.

navel
Artists have debated for hundreds of years whether Adam should be painted with a navel or without one.

navigation
The Greek navigator, Pytheas, discovered the means of calculating latitude in 330 BC. The compass was in common use by AD 1280, and the earliest surviving naval chart dates from 1311.

navy
The beginnings of the Royal Navy were as far back as AD 895 when King Alfred raised a fleet to defend Britain from Viking attacks.

needle
The scale used to grade the size of needles is also used for fishing hooks.

negress
The winner of the first beauty contest held in Belgium in 1888 was a negress.

neighbour
Our nearest star neighbour is roughly 40,230,000km (25,000,000 miles) away.

nerves
Messages are transmitted along the 72·4km (45 miles) of nerves in the human body at up to 402kph (250mph).

nest
The bush-turkey of Australia sometimes builds huge pyramid-shaped nests weighing more than 5 tonnes.

netball
Modern netball players still train by playing games that were popular with the Greeks and Romans. They help to improve ball control and foot work.

New York
The site of New York city was discovered by a Florentine sailor called Giovanni da Verrazano in 1524.

Nick
Old Nick was one of the many names for the devil.

nickname
The nickname given to the Conservative Party, 'Tories', was originally used to describe Irish outlaws in the sixteenth century.

nightingale
Only the cock nightingale sings.

nine
All through the multiplication tables the product of 9 adds up to make 9: $9 \times 5 = 45$, $4 + 5 = 9$, $9 \times 28436 = 255924$, $2 + 5 + 5 + 9 + 2 + 4 = 27$, $2 + 7 = 9$.

nitrogen
More than 10,000,000 tons of nitrogen is put into the earth each year by lightning.

noise
During the artillery bombardment at the beginning of the battle of the Somme in 1916 the noise of the gunfire could be heard in London.

nomad
Nearly all the people living in Western Sahara are nomads.

nose
The famous sixteenth century Danish astrologer Tycho Brahe lost his nose in a duel in 1566, when he was twenty. He wore a replacement gold nose for the rest of his life.

notes
In 1976 notes worth 2,000DM fluttered out of the sky over Limburg in Germany – they were picked up by two clergymen.

novel
Japanese newspapers have been printing a serial from one single novel for over twenty-five years.

November

In the old Roman calendar the year only had ten months and started in March. This meant that what we call November was the ninth month of the Roman year and the Latin word 'novem' in fact means 'nine'.

nuclear

Enrico Fermi achieved the first controlled nuclear reaction at the University of Chicago in 1942.

number

Henry VIII was the first king of England to be given a post nominal number, VIII.

numerals

The numerals we use 1,2,3,4,5 etc. originated in India and came to us by way of the Arabs.

nun

The only food eaten by a German nun, sister Therese Neumann, was the wafer given at mass every morning. She lived on this diet for 35 years, though history does not relate how much she weighed.

nylon

The name 'nylon' was created out of the initials for New York (NY) and London (LON), the two cities in which the synthetic fibre was developed at about the same time.

O

O is the name of a stream on Dartmoor in the south-west of England as well as being the name of a town in Japan.

oak

A mature oak expels seven tonnes of water through its leaves in a day.

oars

Early men were using oars to propel their boats in the north of England 8,000 years ago.

oath

People who wish to read in the Bodleian Library in Oxford take an oath in which they promise not to kindle a fire in the library.

oboe

Musicians consider the oboe to be the most difficult instrument to play correctly.

observatory

For thousands of years, men have been fascinated by the stars. The first observatory was probably erected at Babylon in 2350 BC, and today there are observatories all over the world. Because of the conditions required for using modern telescopes, most observatories have to be built away from large cities and have to be as high up as possible. The High Altitude Observatory of the University of Denver in the USA is 4,297m (14,100ft) above sea level.

ocean

The Pacific Ocean covers a larger area than all the land surfaces of the earth added together.

octopus

Many people believe that a giant octopus was responsible for the sinking of a schooner weighing 150 tonnes in the Bay of Bengal in 1874.

offence

Eating snakes on a Sunday is an offence in Iraq.

officer

Officers in the Royal Navy were not obliged to wear uniforms until 1748.

oil

4·54 litres (1gal) of oil has the same heating power as 0·25cu m (9·14cu ft) of wood.

Olympic Games

The first recorded Olympic Games was held in 776 BC. It consisted of a 200yd foot race.

omelette

You can make an omelette big enough to feed twelve men with an ostrich egg.

omen

Sneezing was believed to be a favourable omen among the Greeks and Romans.

O

one
The number 1 was a symbol of life and of the creative spirit in ancient Egypt.

onion
The onion belongs to the same plant family as the lily.

open-cast
Almost one-third of the coal mined in the USA is obtained by open-cast mining.

opera
Mozart wrote his opera *Don Giovanni* at one sitting. It was performed in public without rehearsal the day after it was written.

orange
An orange tree in France lived and bore fruit for over 470 years.

orbit
The Arend-Roland comet only orbits once in 10,000 years.

orchestra
During the middle ages in China many concerts were given by huge orchestras with hundreds of musicians. In 1872 Johann Strauss, the younger, conducted an orchestra of 987 musicians in Boston, USA – there were 400 first violins.

organ
The organ of the Liverpool Anglican Cathedral has over 9,700 pipes.

ostrich
The ostrich is not only the fastest running bird on land, it is also a strong swimmer.

otter
The otter is the largest carnivorous mammal living in British rivers and lakes.

ounce
We contain 28·35g (1oz) of salt and 14·17g of sugar (·5oz).

overseas

The shortest overseas crossing between two continents is that across the Bosphorus. In Istanbul, Turkey, you can cross from Europe to Asia by ferry in under ten minutes.

overweight

The population of the USA tends to be rather overweight. Altogether Americans carry about 2,000,000 tonnes of surplus fat.

owe

By 1796 the Prince of Wales, later George IV, owed the modern equivalent of £12,000,000 in debts.

owl

At night a barn owl can see a hundred times better than a human being.

oxygen

Divers have found that if they breathe pure oxygen for half-an-hour before their descent, it is possible to hold their breath underwater for thirteen minutes.

P

P was used in medieval Latin as a numeral for 400. As an abbreviation P is helpful to all road users. It stands for Car Park as well as Pedestrian Crossing.

P

painter
Before becoming a world famous novelist William Faulkner worked as a house-painter.

palace
There are 602 rooms in Buckingham Palace, London.

paper
The first paper was invented by Ts'ai Lun in China, in AD 107.

parachuting
In 1797 André-Jacques Garnerin jumped from a balloon over Paris and floated 680m (2,230ft) to the ground by parachute. In 1956 an American marine jumped from a higher altitude but took rather longer to come down. Because of air currents which kept blowing him up, it took him forty minutes to reach the ground.

parsley
There are 2,000 species of parsley. Throughout history it has been attributed with special powers. The ancient Greeks used it to crown winning athletes, Englishmen in the seventeenth century believed that parsley thrown into fish ponds would cure sick fish, and today people eat a sprig of parsley to take away the smell of garlic.

pasta
Spaghetti, macaroni, tortellini, in fact all the pasta we associate with Italy, was first made in China, from rice and bean flour. Marco Polo brought the recipe back to Italy when he returned from China in the thirteenth century.

patron saint
St. Augustine of Hippo is the patron saint of brewers, the patron saint of librarians is St. Jerome, and St. William is the patron saint of hatters.

pencil
There is enough carbon in the human body to make the leads of 9,000 pencils.

perfume
Roman ladies used a paste made from vinegar and chalk as a perfume and deodorant.

periscope
When Charles Lindbergh made the first solo flight across the Atlantic in 1927 the fuel tanks on his plane 'The Spirit of St. Louis' were so large that he had to look through a periscope to see over them.

pesticide
Even in the ancient world men realized the value of toxic chemicals in protecting their crops from pests. The Greek poet Homer mentions the use of burning sulphur.

pet
Each year the British spend twice as much money on pet food as they spend on baby food.

petrol
Every day the world uses 4,546,000,000 litres (1,000,000,000 gallons) of petrol.

phantom
When King George V was serving as a young naval officer he saw the famous phantom sailing ship known as *The Flying Dutchman* in the south Atlantic.

P

pigeon
Racing pigeons have been measured flying at speeds well over 160kph (100mph).

pillar-box
The use of pillar-boxes was introduced by a well-known English novelist of the nineteenth century, Anthony Trollope.

pillows
The ancient Egyptians must have had difficulty going to sleep – they used pillows made out of stone.

plague
Even before the Great Plague of 1665, over 75,400 inhabitants of London had died of the disease in the previous sixty years. In fact between 1603 and 1665 there had only been four separate years in which London had been completely free from plague.

plastic
Even ships are made of plastic nowadays. In 1972 the Royal Navy's first plastic warship came into operation; she is called *HMS Wilton*.

platform
There is a station platform in Bengal, India which is 833m (911yds) long.

playing-card
Historians believe that playing cards were invented in China in about AD 1120. Card games were so popular in England by the reign of Edward IV (1461–1470) that an Act of Parliament was passed forbidding the import of foreign cards.

Pluto
Pluto is the coldest planet in our universe because it is the farthest from the sun, which is about 5,913,514,000km (3,674,488,000 miles) away. Scientists reckon that the surface temperature is −220°C (−360°F).

plywood
Plywood was invented by Immanuel Nobel, the father of Alfred Nobel who made a fortune from his own invention of dynamite.

poetry
When he was a schoolboy Thomas Chatterton taught himself medieval English and then used it to write poems by an imaginary medieval monk. The poems were so good that scholars and experts believed they were genuine for over a hundred years.

poison
Cleopatra, ancient queen of Egypt, used to test the efficiency of her poisons on her servants.

pole
There are 179 days of continuous sunlight at the South Pole while for the same time the sun is not seen at the North Pole at all. 450,000,000 years ago the earth was positioned in a different way in relation to its present axis and the South Pole was in the area of what is now the Sahara.

polo
The fourteenth century Mongol conqueror Tamerlane used to play polo with the skulls of those he had killed in battle.

Pope
Benedict IX was created Pope when he was twelve.

population
Nearly 40 percent of the Third World is under fifteen years old. Almost one-quarter of the world's people live in China, and it is estimated that there will be 1,800,000,000 Chinese in the year 2000.

porridge
Originally porridge was a thick vegetable soup.

portrait
The official portrait of the Duke of Monmouth was painted after his execution in 1685. The head had to be sewn back onto the body which was then dressed and posed for the artist to copy.

post
In 1685 the postal service moved letters and parcels at approximately 8kph (5mph) in England.

P

pouch
Anteaters, koalas, kangaroos and sea horses all have pouches.

prediction
The invention of cars, aeroplanes, telescopes and bombs were all predicted by a thirteenth century English monk Roger Bacon, who was the first person to experiment with lenses for magnifying objects.

president
Since 1840 every president of the USA elected in a year ending with 0 has died in office. The most recent was J. F. Kennedy elected in 1960.

princess
A Tartar princess of the thirteenth century called Aiyavuk ('Shining Moon') was a formidable wrestler. She used to wrestle with every man who wanted to marry her and took a forfeit of 100 horses from them when they failed to beat her. By the time she was thirty she had acquired 10,000 horses.

printing
When Wang Chieh made the first printed book in China in AD 848 he had to carve each page on a separate block of wood.

prisoner
The last prisoner to be held in the Tower of London was the Nazi leader Rudolf Hess who was imprisoned there during World War Two.

propeller
Most ships are propelled by screw propellers today. The first one was used in 1838; in 1863 the first use was made of twin screw propellers, and in 1967 a fifty-three ton propeller was made for a tanker in Germany. It measured 9·29m (30·5ft) in diameter.

protein
The people of Canada, USA, New Zealand and Australia eat roughly twenty times as much animal protein a day as the people of India.

puck
Ice hockey is one of the fastest games in the world. When hit hard the puck can shoot across the ice at a speed of 189kph (117·5mph).

punch
The American boxer Sugar Ray Robinson can throw a punch at 56kph (35mph).

pumping
Cockles and razor shells both eat by pumping water through their shells and straining the food from it.

purple
Roman senators used to wear a purple stripe in their togas as an indication of their official status.

pyramid
The Great Pyramid of Cheops which was built in 2580 BC is 146·6m (480·9ft) high. It was the highest structure in the world for 4,000 years until the central tower of Lincoln Cathedral passed it in 1548 with a height of 160m (525ft).

Q

Q
Q is the least used letter in the English alphabet.

quadruplets
The chances of a mother giving birth to quadruplets, four babies born at the same time, are about one in 600,000.

quagga
This is not a word you will hear a lot, but it is very useful if you want to impress anyone with your knowledge. A quagga was a rare zebra which only had stripes on the front of its body. It became extinct in 1882.

quail
The quail is the smallest game bird found in Britain. A flock of quail should really be called a 'bevy'.

quaker
When the non-conformist preacher George Fox was arrested in the seventeenth century he said to the magistrate: 'You should quake at the name of the Lord when you mention it.' Since that time his followers have been called Quakers.

quarantine
During an outbreak of the plague in London, Queen Elizabeth I retreated to Windsor for safety. Anyone who broke the quarantine regulations and entered Windsor from the capital was ordered to be hanged in the market place.

quarter
One quarter of the forests in the world are in Siberia.

quatorzes
Quatorze means fourteen in French. Since many hostesses believed that it was unlucky to sit thirteen guests at a dinner table they used to hire an extra guest to make the number up to fourteen. These people became so popular that they established a profession known as the 'quatorzes'.

queen
Lady Jane Grey was queen of England for only nine days.

quipu
2,000 years ago ancient Peruvians counted by means of coloured strings with knots. They called them quipus.

R
When R is used as an abbreviation in connection with royalty it stands for one of two Latin words: 'rex' a king or 'regina' a queen. Whenever you see the initials E.R. they represent Elizabeth Regina, or Queen Elizabeth.

rabbit
The maximum recorded life of a rabbit is eighteen years.

racecourse
Although there are accounts of races between two horses dating from the fourteenth century, the first permanent racecourse in England was not established until 1540, at Chester.

rail
Railed tracks were being used in mines in Alsace as early as 1550.

railway
The Japanese National Railway network carries 17,000,000 passengers a day.

rain
Almost one eighth of the earth's surface receives less than 25cm (9·8ins) of rain a year.

raisin
If you drop a raisin into a glass of champagne it will continually float up and down from the bottom of the glass to the top.

rat
A rat can survive longer without water than a camel.

rattlesnake
In the state of Florida rattlesnake meat is served as an hors d'oeuvres.

razor
In 1903 the American Safety Razor Company sold only fifty-one razors and 168 blades. A year later the sales improved and they sold 90,000 razors and 12,400,000 blades.

rebellion
Between 20,000,000 and 30,000,000 people died during the thirteen year Taiping rebellion, which took place in China during the nineteenth century. The leader, Hsin-Chi'uan, believed he was the reincarnation of Jesus Christ.

reciting
Richard Porson the famous eighteenth century scholar had an incredible memory. He could recite all twelve books of *Paradise Lost* forwards and backwards from memory.

red
Many Hindu women stain their teeth red because they believe it improves their appearance.

regiment
The Royal Scots are the oldest regular regiment in the British army. They were first raised in 1633.

reign
A sixth dynasty pharaoh of Egypt, Pepi II, reigned for ninety-four years.

religion
England was joined to the Church of Rome in 664 at the Synod of Whitby. The two religions were separated again 870 years later, when Henry VIII created himself Supreme Head of the Church in England.

rent
The Earl of Stirling rented the whole of Canada from James I of Scotland for one penny a year.

reporter
Karl Marx worked as a newspaper reporter in London in 1848.

reptile
The Stegosaurus lived about 150,000,000 years ago during the Age of Reptiles. It weighed 1·75 tonnes, was 9m (30ft) in length yet its brain was only the size of a walnut.

restaurant
In fifty years as a restaurant grader, Fred Magel has eaten in nearly 40,000 restaurants around the world.

revolution
Rearranged, the letters of 'revolution' give the anagram 'love to ruin'.

rhinoceros
It takes 560 days for a rhinoceros calf to be born.

rhubarb
Rhubarb gets its name from the Greek name for the river Volga. 'Rha' was the name of the river and 'barb' means 'uncultivated'. Therefore rhubarb was a wild plant growing beside the river Volga.'

R

ribs
Horses have eighteen pairs of ribs, humans have twelve.

rickshaw
An American baptist minister invented the rickshaw in Yokohama, Japan, in 1869.

riding
When George IV was still Prince of Wales he once rode from London to Brighton and back on horseback in ten hours.

river
The Kingdom of Saudi Arabia covers an area of 2,149,690sq km (830,000sq miles) and yet there are no rivers in the entire country.

road
Roads were only developed 1,000 years after the invention of the wheeled transport vehicle. The first road network was created in China around 2,700 BC.

robin
Experiments made with robins have shown that each bird ate 4·26m (14ft) of worms in twenty-four hours and in twelve hours a robin eats more than 41 per cent of its own body weight.

rocket
Sir William Congreve invented iron-cased rockets filled with gunpowder. The first rocket powered by liquid fuel flew in 1926.

round the world
The first ship to sail round the world was the Spanish galleon *Victoria* in 1519–1522. She was commanded by Ferdinand Magellan and later by Sebastian del Cano. In 1957, three US bombers flew round the world non-stop in forty-five hours, nineteen minutes.

rubber
The great far-eastern rubber estates in Ceylon and Singapore were founded from seeds grown at Kew Gardens, near London.

rum
From 1692–1948 the alcohol level in Royal Navy rum was 79·8 percent. It was then reduced to 46·3 percent before the issue of rum was finally abolished in 1970.

running
In 1915 Noah Young ran 1·6km (1 mile) in 8·25 minutes carrying a man weighing 68kg (10st 10lb).

rust
After a building in Ohio had been built on a layer of iron pyrites the mineral was exposed to the elements and began to form rust. The rust formed so quickly that in fifteen years it had lifted the basement floors 38·10cm (15in), 2·54cm (1in) a year.

S

S is derived from a letter in the Phoenician alphabet that was shaped like our W.

sack
Sack was the Elizabethan name for what we call sherry. Sack is mentioned more often in Shakespeare's plays than all the other wines added together.

safety-pin
Safety-pins were being used in the Mediterranean lands in the Bronze Age.

sailing
Clare Francis is the fastest woman to sail single-handed across the Atlantic. She made the crossing in just over twenty-nine days in 1976.

salt
The Dead Sea is over six times as salty as the Atlantic Ocean.

sandwich
The sandwich is named after the eighteenth-century fourth Earl of Sandwich. He would often remain at the gambling table during normal meal times and instructed his servant to bring him a slice of meat between two pieces of bread.

S

sardines
Sardines are less expensive than the oil in which they are packed, which may explain why they are so tightly packed in the tin.

sardine tin
A legendary Italian film star called Maciste could open a sardine tin by squeezing it with his fingers.

Saturday
All the British monarchs from Queen Anne until George IV died on Saturdays.

sauna bath
There are over 500,000 sauna baths in Finland.

scarlet
The last time that British troops wore scarlet uniforms in battle was during the Ashanti campaign of 1895–96.

school
The word school comes from the ancient Greek word 'skhole', which means leisure.

screwdriver
The screwdriver was invented before the screw. It was used to extract twisted nails.

sculptures
The white sculptures which we are so used to seeing in collections of Greek and Roman art were once gaily decorated with paint and inlaid accessories.

sea
Over 70 percent of the earth's surface is covered by sea.

sea battle
In the four-day battle of the Coral Sea in 1942 all the fighting was carried out by aeroplanes.

seals
Baby seals are always born on land and have to be taught how to swim.

sediment
One of the purposes of the indentation in the bottom of wine bottles is to trap the sediment in the wine. The other is to strengthen the bottle.

seed-drill
Jethro Tull, the inventor of the seed-drill, was a musician and a lawyer.

September
September used to be the seventh month of the old year and is named after the Latin word for seven which is 'septem'.

sewage
Although the palace of Versailles had magnificent fountains and water gardens when it was first built, there were no sewage facilities or bathrooms.

shaving
A man shaves about 27·4m (30yds) of whiskers off his face during his lifetime.

sheep
There are eleven sheep to every person in Australia and over twenty sheep per person in New Zealand.

sheet
When sailors talk about 'sheets', they are not referring to the sheets that go onto a bed or even to sails; they mean ropes.

shells
Seashells have been found in rocks high up in the Himalayan mountains which prove that at one time the highest mountains in the world once formed the sea-floor.

ship
When the *Great Eastern* was launched in 1858 she was six times larger than any other ship afloat at the time.

shooting stars
Shooting stars are caused by tiny particles entering the earth's atmosphere and causing a luminous effect as they burn up.

S

shorthand
The principles of modern shorthand were developed by the ancient Egyptians.

short sight
King George III was notoriously short-sighted.

shrink
After the age of forty the human body begins to shrink. You might not notice, however, as it takes ten years to shrink 1 cm.

side light
Before electric lights were installed in cars they carried side lights that burnt oil.

side saddle
The side saddle was developed for Anne of Bohemia, the Queen of King Richard II.

Sikh
Every member of the Indian religious sect of the Sikhs is called 'Singh', which means lion-hearted.

singe
Roman men did not go to the barber to have their hair cut, they used to have it singed.

skateboard
Champion skateboarders can reach speeds of over 91 kph (56mph).

skating
In 1975 Yevgeniy Kulikov skated at a speed of 47·36kph (29·43mph).

skeleton
More than half the bones in the human skeleton are in the wrists, ankles, hands and feet.

skin
The complete skin covering the human body would cover an area of about 1·85sq m (20sq ft) and it would weigh 2·72kg (6lb) when bundled together.

skipping
J. Rogers of Melbourne, Australia, once skipped 286 times in one minute, averaging 4·76 turns each second.

sky scraper
The first building called a sky scraper was the Home Insurance building in Chicago, which was built in 1885.

slaves
Pope Paul III decreed that all Englishmen who supported Henry VIII should be made slaves.

sleep
The mimosa is a plant which appears to go to sleep at night. It folds its leaves which then become quite brittle and can be broken off easily. In the morning they open up and become supple again.

sleep walking
An Argentinian waiter, Carlos Diaz, was walking home from work one evening when he suddenly became unconscious. His last memory was of being drawn up by a paralysing beam of light. When he woke up four hours later he found himself 804km (500 miles) away from home.

S

sloth
The three-toed sloth is the slowest moving land mammal.
Its average speed 1·8–2·4m (6–8ft) per minute is slower
than that of a tortoise, which is the slowest reptile.

slot machine
The first coin operated slot machine was designed by an
ancient Egyptian called Ctesibius, in about 200 BC. It
was used for supplying holy water at a temple in
Alexandria.

smell
The emperor moth can smell a female of the same species
up to 11km (6·8 miles) away.

smoking
There is a law in New York which prevents women from
smoking in public and which has never been repealed.

snake
A snake has no ears but it uses its tongue to pick up
vibrations in the air, so in a way it hears with its tongue.

sneeze
It is impossible to sneeze and keep your eyes open at the
same time.

snoring
Medical evidence suggests that we snore less during those
periods of sleep when we are dreaming.

snow
More snow falls in the state of Virginia, USA, than in the
Arctic lowlands.

snowplough
The government of the desert state of Dubai bought a
snowplough in 1975, although no snow ever falls there.
They use it for clearing sand off roads.

soap
The British use almost twice as much soap per person as
the Dutch.

soda water
There is no soda in soda water.

solo
The first man to row solo across the Pacific Ocean was Anders Svedland from Sweden. In 1974 he rowed from Chile to Samoa in 118 days.

sound
The speed of sound at sea level, at 0°C, is 1,194kph (742mph).

speed
The world land-speed record has twice been broken by steam-powered cars.

speech
Raymond Glendenning, a BBC commentator, once spoke 176 words in thirty seconds.

speedometer
Speedometers were not made compulsory in cars until 1927.

spider
You would need to collect 27,000 spiders' webs in order to make 453·6g (1lb) of web.

sponge
A sponge is really a colony of thousands of little creatures.

squirrel
Red squirrels attract more fleas than any other animal.

stamp
During his lifetime King George V collected 325 albums full of stamps.

star
The most distant star from earth belonging to our galaxy is 75,000 light years away.

station
There is a railway station in Bolivia which is 4,786m (15,702ft) above sea level.

steak
When the first piece of steak arrived in the gold-rush town of Circle City, Alaska, it was auctioned and sold for £24 per pound.

S

steamboat
The first steamboat designed by Denis Papin in 1707 was destroyed by a mob.

stirrups
Assyrian warriors used stirrups in the ninth century BC but it took 1,500 years before they reappeared again in Europe.

stocks
Lawmakers in British Columia once felt that anyone who bought an ice-cream or a bag of peanuts should spend two hours in the stocks.

stomach
A cow has four stomachs.

strawberry
Strawberries are very useful for cleaning your teeth and for relieving sunburn on your face.

stump
Australian fast bowler, Albert Cotter, broke more than twenty cricket stumps during his cricketing career.

submarine
In 1620 a Dutch scientist, Cornelius van Drebbel, gave a demonstration of his 'submarine' in England. This craft consisted of a rowing boat covered with leather which moved along under water.

suicide
According to official figures there is one suicide attempt every twenty minutes in the USA.

sun
The sun contains 99·87 per cent of the mass in our solar system. You would need 1,000,000 earths to make a ball as large as the sun.

sunspots
Huge storms on the surface of the sun are called sunspots. In 1947 a sunspot which occurred measured 18,129,000,000sq km (7,000,000,000sq miles).

surgeon
The German romantic poet, Friedrich von Schiller, was originally an army surgeon.

surname
William Shakespeare spelt his own surname in eleven different ways.

survivor
Rescuers found one survivor in the town of St. Pierre, on the French Caribbean island of Martinique, following the devastating earthquake of 1908. The lucky man was a short-term prisoner in the town's prison.

suspension
Even before 1580 passenger coaches had spring suspension.

swallow
Babies can breathe and swallow at the same time, adults cannot.

sweat
Dogs sweat through their paws.

sword
The sword used by Edward III was so large that it required two normal men to lift it.

symphony
Havergal Brian was ninety-one when he wrote his Symphony No. 30.

T
T stands for the 'tesla', the unit which measures magnetic flux density.

table tennis
The earliest trade name for table tennis was 'Gossima'. In 1958, Joy Foster became the singles and doubles champion of Jamaica at the age of eight.

tail
The kinkajou of South America has a tail twice as long as its body. When it goes to sleep at night it wraps itself up in its tail and uses it as a pillow.

tailor

The Indian tailor bird gets its name from the way in which it makes its nests. It takes a large leaf and then sews the sides together with fibre until the leaf is nest-shaped, using its beak as a needle.

talc

On the Moh's Hardness Scale, talc is given the value of one because it is the softest mineral on the scale and can be crushed with your finger nail. At the other end of the scale is diamond which has a value of ten because it is the hardest mineral on the scale.

tank

The first tank track was designed by a lieutenant in the Royal Naval Air Service.

tapestry

The Bayeux tapestry, which illustrates scenes from the Norman conquest, is 70·4 m (231 ft) long.

tarantula

The tarantula is one of the few spiders that cannot spin a web.

tattoo

A Canadian tattoo artist, 'Sailor' Joe Simmons, advertised his trade by having his own body decorated with 4,831 tattoos.

tax

A special tax was levied on beards during the reign of Peter the Great in Russia.

tea
Up until 200 years ago blocks of tea were used as money in Siberia.

teddy bear
Teddy bears are named after the American president Theodore Roosevelt.

teeth
We have twenty-two teeth in our first set, called milk teeth, and thirty-two in the second permanent set.

teething
Louis XIV, Richard III, and Napoleon Bonaparte all began teething long before most babies. They were born with several teeth already formed.

telephone
Even by 1976 there was still no telephone service in the Himalayan kingdom of Bhutan.

telescope
The first man to use lenses in a telescope was a thirteenth century English monk called Roger Bacon.

television
The first public demonstration of television was given in 1926. The first television broadcasting station opened ten years later at Alexandra Palace in London.

temperature
It is a mistake to believe that it always becomes colder when you travel farther north. New York lies further south than anywhere in Britain and yet it has a lower average temperature than Reykjavik, the capital of Iceland. Reykjavik is only just below the Arctic Circle.

tennis
Modern lawn tennis owes its origins to a game played by French monks in their monastery cloisters in the eleventh century.

tern
Every year the Arctic Tern flies from the Arctic right round the world to the Antarctic and then back again.

thatch
In many parts of Asia buildings are thatched with rice-straw.

the
'The' is *the* most frequently used word in *the* English language. See what I mean?

theatre
Charles II was the first British monarch to attend a public theatre.

thieves
St. Nicholas is the patron saint of thieves.

third
'Lucky September 3', Oliver Cromwell must have thought after he had won two great battles at Dunbar and Worcester on that date. Unfortunately it also turned out to be the day on which he died.

throne
The Indian emperor, Shah Jehan, spent an estimated £6,000,000 on a magnificent throne. It was 1·82m (6ft) long and 1·22m (4ft) wide, made of solid gold, inlaid with jewels and covered by a solid gold canopy fringed with pearls.

throw
Ericus, the second king of Denmark, could throw a spear farther when he was sitting down than other men could throw standing up.

thumbs
A gymnast called Bob Jones could do a thumb-stand, supporting his own weight upside down on his thumbs. What made his feat really spectacular was that he used to balance in this position on top of a pair of Indian clubs.

thunder
In 1930 it was reported in Germany that five men covered in layers of ice had fallen out of a thunder cloud onto the Rhön mountains.

tight-rope
On one occasion the French tight-rope walker, Charles Blondin, cooked an omelette when he was performing on a tight-rope suspended over the Niagara Falls.

tigress
Colonel Jim Corbett shot a tigress in India in 1907 after reports that she had killed over 400 people.

tin
Over half the tins in the world are made and used in the USA.

tip
This word so beloved of waiters and porters is in fact an abbreviation of three words: To Insure Promptness.

title
Muhammad Ali is the first boxer ever to regain the world heavy-weight title twice.

T

toads
A freak storm of thousands of small toads rained down on the village of Brignoles, France, in 1973.

tobacco
The first woman in Europe to take tobacco was Catherine of Medici. She did not smoke but used it in her snuff.

tobogganing
The British were the first to develop the sport of tobogganing in the nineteenth century. In 1975 Poldi Berchtold of Switzerland reached a speed of 145kph (90mph) when he descended the famous Cresta Run by toboggan.

toe
The religious tradition of kissing the Pope's toe lasted for over 1,000 years until it was eventually abolished in 1773.

ton
The average person eats and drinks about one tonne of food and drink every year.

tongue
The tongue of a chameleon is several inches longer than its body. It shoots out this very long tongue to catch insects.

torpedo
The US navy has started recovering torpedoes lost in deep water by sending trained whales down to retrieve them.

tortoise
Greek historians claim that the great playwright Aeschylus died after being hit on the head by a tortoise dropped by a passing eagle.

Tower of London
Henry III used the Tower as a zoo as well as a prison.
He kept a pet elephant there after it had been presented
to him by the King of France.

track
There is a section of railway track in Australia which
runs in a straight line across the Nullarbor Plain for
478km (297 miles).

traffic lights
There is a set of traffic lights controlling the junction of
two canals in Venice.

transatlantic
The first transatlantic crossing by hot air balloon was
made by three American balloonists in the summer of
1978.

transfusion
The first blood transfusions given were with animal
blood.

translation
Don Quixote has been translated more widely than any
other book except the Bible.

trial
In ancient British trials the suspect was made to swallow
a slice of bread and cheese.

triplets
Between 1849 and 1957 parents who gave birth to triplets
were entitled to receive a Royal payment of £3.00.

trouble
The Chinese character for 'trouble' shows two women
under one roof.

trout
A breed of trout which is slightly different from either the
river or sea trout is called the 'slob trout'. It lives in
estuaries.

T

truck
Before 1920 it was unusual for trucks to move faster than 15kph (9·3mph).

trumpet
Trumpets were being played in ancient Denmark as early as 1760 BC.

trunk
An elephant can hold 9 litres (2 gallons) of water in its trunk.

truth
In order to see if Bedouin Arabs were telling the truth they were often made to lick a red-hot bar of metal. Their tongues were only burnt if they were lying.

tulip
Although the tulip is usually associated with the Netherlands it originated in Turkey. The name 'tulip' comes from the Turkish word for a turban.

tuna
The tuna belongs to the same fish family as the mackerel.

tunnel
The tunnels on the London Underground Northern Line, between East Finchley and Morden via the Bank, have a total length of 27·85km (17·3 miles).

turbans
Many of the tribesmen in Afghanistan wear turbans 6·09m (20ft) long.

Turkey
Turkey is the only country in the world situated in two continents and separated by sea.

turtles
Turtles have no teeth.

tutor
It is little wonder that Alexander was 'Great'; his tutor was none other than the legendary philosopher Aristotle.

twins
Twins are born more frequently in the western part of the world than in the eastern part.

typhoon
The word for a typhoon is similar in several eastern languages: 'Taafuna' is the god of storms in Polynesian, 'Ty-fong' is a violent rain storm in Chinese and in Arabic 'Tyfoon' means a whirlwind.

typing
In 1918 Margaret Owen of New York achieved a typing speed of 170 words per minute on a manual machine. This was calculated by deducting a ten word penalty for each mistake she made.

tyre
The first successful tubeless tyres for cars were made in 1948, and the first radial tyres were made by the Michelin company in 1953.

U
U is the name of a place in the Caroline Islands in the Pacific Ocean.

ulcers
Three or four times as many men get ulcers as women.

umbrella
The first steel-framed umbrellas appeared in 1852.

unconsciousness
Elaine Esposito of Florida, USA, was unconscious between 1941 and 1978 when she died.

underarm
Until the first quarter of the nineteenth century all cricket deliveries were bowled underarm.

undergraduate
Lord Kelvin, the well known Scottish mathematician, became an undergraduate at Glasgow University when he was just over ten years old.

U

underground
The oldest underground railway in the world is a stretch of the Metropolitan Line between Bishop's Road and Farringdon, in London. It was opened in 1863.

underwater
Polynesian divers on the island of Tonga used to hold underwater walking races.

unemployment
Switzerland has the lowest unemployment level in the world. At the beginning of 1974 there were only eighty-one registered unemployed people in Switzerland.

uniforms
King George V was entitled to wear more than a hundred military and naval uniforms.

Union Jack
In 1964 the Canadian national flag was changed. The red ensign, which displayed the Union Jack, was replaced by the Maple Leaf which does not show the British flag.

United Nations
The official languages of the United Nations are Chinese, English, French, Russian and Spanish.

Universe
The universe is between 17·5,000,000 and 21·3,000,000 years old, according to astronomical calculations.

university
The oldest university in the world was probably the college Alexander the Great founded at Alexandria in the fourth century BC. The oldest university in Europe is the University of Salerno in Italy, founded in AD 850.

Uranus
The fifth satellite of Uranus was not discovered until 1948.

USSR
The USSR is larger than the whole continent of South America. In fact it covers one-sixth of the total land area of the earth.

V
V is an abbreviation for 'victory' and the symbol for the unit of electric potential, 'volt'. It is also the Roman numeral for five.

vacuum
If a lead weight and a feather were dropped inside a vacuum they would fall at exactly the same rate.

vacuum flask
The mother-in-law of Sir William Dewer, inventor of the vacuum flask, doubted its efficiency, so she knitted a woolly cosy to fit over it and retain the heat.

Van cat
This is a breed of cat found in Turkey which is fond of swimming. Most cats hate water.

V

vapour
Drops of water that are dropped or thrown onto a very hot surface, like a stove, do not actually touch the surface. They always rest on a cushion of vapour until they boil away and disappear.

vegetarians
All Romans were vegetarians until the time of the Caesars.

veins
Frederick the Great, King of Prussia 1740–1786, used to have his veins cut open to let out blood at the height of many of his battles. He claimed that the treatment helped to calm his nerves.

velocity
Scientists estimate that when the US Space Shuttle Orbiter comes into operation flying outside the atmosphere it will reach a velocity of 28,325kph (17,600mph).

venom
One gram of venom from a king cobra is enough to kill 150 people.

verses
There are 158 verses in the Greek national anthem.

vessels
If all the blood vessels in the human body were laid end to end they would stretch 160,930km (100,000 miles).

vestiphobia
Vestiphobia is a fear of clothing.

Victory
Nelson's flagship HMS *Victory* carried a crew of 850 men.

Vikings
The Vikings discovered America almost 500 years before Christopher Columbus.

vinegar
When Hannibal was crossing the Alps he found his path blocked by an enormous rock. The only way of breaking the rock was to heat it with a giant fire and then pour vinegar onto it. Once it was red hot, it could be cracked by striking it with iron rods. Without vinegar the Carthaginian army might never have passed the obstacle and Italy would never have been invaded.

violinist
Yehudi Menhuin, perhaps the greatest living violinist, gave his first public concert when he was eight, and first appeared in *Who's Who* at the age of fifteen.

vision
In 1871, five children in a French village independently described a vision which lasted for three-and-three-quarter hours. They saw a beautiful woman hovering above them, and spelt out religious messages as they appeared in the sky.

vitamins
Apart from human beings, apes and guinea pigs are the only mammals capable of producing vitamin C in their own bodies.

vocabulary
The English language has a vocabulary of about 800,000 words. In normal speech we use about 2,000, medical students add about 10,000 extra words to their vocabularies during their studies and Shakespeare used 15,000 in his plays and poetry.

vodka
In 1947 a Russian workman died after what appeared to be an internal explosion, which was caused by blowing out a match after drinking a great deal of vodka.

V

voice
The first animals to have voices were the earliest four-legged amphibians. The alligator, a modern amphibian, has a bellow which can be heard 1·6km (1 mile) away.

volcano
The eruption of the volcano Krakatoa in 1883 was so violent that the noise could be heard over 4,800km (3,000 miles) away in Bangkok. The dust from the eruption covered almost every part of the globe and for the next two years it formed a thin haze which could be seen in the sky at sunsets as far away as London.

vole
The female meadow vole can reproduce only twenty-five days after her own birth. She can give birth to up to seventeen litters a year, each one consisting of six–eight young.

volleyball
Volleyball was first developed for middle-aged members of the American YMCA.

voltage
A bolt of lightning can hit the earth with a charge of up to 100,000,000 volts and experts calculate that lightning hits the earth a hundred times every second.

volume
The volume of water in the river Amazon is greater than the total combined volume of the next eight largest rivers in the world.

vowels
In Arabic, vowels are not counted as letters, and in writing they are indicated by signs which are often not included in newspaper printing.

voyage
The total cost of Christopher Columbus's voyage of discovery to America was a little over £3,500, the cost of a medium priced car today.

W

W was not used by the Romans in their alphabet; they made do with V. As an abbreviation W is used in science to represent the unit of power and radiant flux, the 'watt'.

waist

Slim waists have always been admired, but sometimes the demands of fashion have been rather extreme. In the seventeenth century Louis XIV's queen succeeded in reducing her vital statistic to 33cm (13in), and at about 1860 it was generally accepted that 43–53cm (17–21in) was a desirable waist measurement.

walking

At Newmarket, in 1809, Captain Barclay succeeded in walking 1,000 miles (1,609km) in 1,000 hours. This feat lasted day and night for six weeks.

wall

The Great Wall of China stretches for 6,230km (3,930 miles) along the old northern frontier. It was used as a line of defence for 1,700 years and during the Middle Ages many of the guards were born on the wall, spent all their lives patrolling it and were finally buried beside it, without ever having left.

wallpaper

Wallpaper first appeared as a decoration in rooms at about 1645.

war

In 1944 the cost of World War Two reached its peak for the British government. At one time they were spending over £1,000,000,000 a week.

watch

The first pocket watch was invented in 1509 in Nuremburg by Peter Henlein. Because of its shape it was called the Nuremburg Egg.

W

water
The English novelist, Arnold Bennett, died of typhoid in Paris in 1931, after drinking a glass of water. He had been trying to prove that the local water was perfectly safe to drink.

water-closet
One of the first people to make use of a WC was Queen Elizabeth I who had one installed in Richmond Palace in 1596. However, it was almost 200 years before their use became a general practice.

waterfalls
Over 322,000,000 litres (71,000,000 gallons) of water flow over the Victoria Falls in Africa every minute.

water-mill
According to the Domesday Book, compiled in 1086, there were 5,264 water-mills in England.

weasels
The Romans used weasels to catch mice just as we use cats.

weaving
The ancient Egyptians were the first people to weave cloth to make clothing; the ancient Chinese were the first to weave silk, and the first reference to weaving in England records it in York in 1331.

wedding
There were thirty-four separate wedding celebrations when Henry II of France married Catherine de Medici in 1533.

week-day
Wednesday is named after Woden the Anglo-Saxon god of victory, Friday is named after his wife Frigg the goddess of love, and his sons Tiw, the god of war, and Thor, the god of thunder, give their names to Tuesday and Thursday respectively.

weight
The average man weighs roughly forty times as much as his own brain.

well
You can see the stars from the bottom of a well, even in daylight.

wellingtons
Rubber boots were first worn by the Duke of Wellington during the Napoleonic wars. When they came into general use they were named after him.

werewolves
The technical name for werewolves is 'lycanthropes'.

whale
A blue whale calf is born measuring 6·7m (22ft) long and weighing 10 tonnes. In 2·5 years it grows to a length of 22·5m (75ft) and becomes sexually mature.

wheel
The ancient civilizations of the Aztecs, the Mayas, the Incas and the Toltecs all existed without using the wheel.

whisker
During the sixteenth and seventeenth centuries in Peking a common way of taking revenge was to put finely chopped tiger whiskers in an enemy's food.

W

whistle
A French aristocrat who whistled at the queen, Marie Antoinette, was arrested and spent fifty years of his life in prison.

widow
Frau Irmgard Brens, who lived in Berlin during the nineteenth century, was widowed six times – all her husbands committed suicide.

wife
In 1832 a farmer in Carlisle sold his wife for twenty shillings and a Newfoundland dog.

window
There is a record of the use of glass in windows on the continent dating from 290 BC, but the earliest mention in England does not appear until 1180.

wine
The Italians drink more wine per person each year than the Austrians drink beer.

wings
A prehistoric flying reptile, the Pteranodon, had a wing span of 9·14m (30ft). The largest wingspan of any modern bird is that of the albatross which measures 2·13m (7ft).

wire
Michael Faraday proved that an electric current could be generated in a loop of wire in 1830.

witch
The last European witch was burned in Switzerland in 1782.

wolf
In 1920 a missionary in Bengal, India, found two little girls in a wolf's den. The children behaved exactly like the animals, who, it appeared, had brought them up.

woman
Queen Hatshepsut who ruled Egypt from 1511–1480 BC was the first great woman to be recorded in history.

wool
Despite the cold climate of northern China, wool has never been used to make knitted garments. Warm clothes are made there by using thick cotton padding to keep out the cold.

words
No more than 6,654 words are used in all the books of the Bible and the Talmud.

world
The first person to claim that the world was round was Pythagoras who lived almost 2,500 years ago.

worthless
The action of estimating something as worthless is called 'floccipaucinihlipilification', it is worth remembering.

wreck
When the oil tanker *Olympic Bravery* ran aground off the French coast on her maiden voyage in 1976, she became the largest wreck in history.

wrestler
In the 1970 Commonwealth Games a twelve-year-old Indian wrestler won a gold medal.

wrist
The human body has eight bones in each wrist.

writing
At the peak of his writing career Frank Richards, creator of Billy Bunter, wrote 80,000 words a week.

written language
The oldest known written language is the Cuneiform script used by the Sumerians, dating from 4240 BC.

X
According to the international code of signal flags, the 'X' flag flying on its own means: 'Stop carrying out your intentions and watch for my signals'.

X-certificate

The British Board of Film Censors only got around to introducing the X-certificate for films in 1951. Up until that time people under sixteen could watch any films.

Xmas

Xmas is an abbreviation for Christmas which should only be used in writing. The X is itself an abbreviation for the Greek word for Christ, which began with an X.

X-rays

The vital discovery of X-rays was made by a German physicist Wilhelm Konrad Röntgen in 1895.

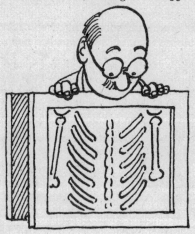

xylophone

Xylophones are to Cuba what tom-toms are to Nigeria, and yet in 1975 a British manufacturer won an order to export a batch of xylophones to Cuba.

Y

There is a village in France called Y.

yacht

The Queen's Royal Yacht *Britannia* can be converted into a hospital ship in time of war. This dual purpose was intended when the ship was originally designed.

yard
In the twelfth century, Henry I decreed that a yard was to equal the distance from the end of his nose to the end of his thumb.

ye
For centuries many people have believed that 'ye' was an old-fashioned form of 'the'. This error arose from the misreading of the Anglo-Saxon word for 'the', which was 'þe'. However, 'ye' did once mean 'you'. So strictly speaking a sign reading 'Ye Olde Thatch Tea-Shop' means 'you old thatch tea-shop'.

year
The year has not always consisted of 365 days. In the ancient civilizations of India, Persia, Babylon and Central America the year was reckoned to consist of only 360 days.

yellow
To scientific researchers working with risky materials the colour for danger is not red, it is bright yellow.

yew
A spear made from yew wood was found at Clacton-on-Sea and was dated by archaeologists as 50,000 years old.

yogurt
Yogurt is a Turkish word.

yolk
Forgers who print false banknotes use egg yolks to give their counterfeits a feel like that of the genuine notes.

yo-yo
Originally the yo-yo was a Filipino jungle weapon.

Z

Z
z is used in meteorology to represent dust or haze (this is a lower case Z not a capital).

zero
The Babylonians only developed a symbol for zero in about 300 BC. They did not write it as we do as 'o', but as ':' instead.

zero, absolute
In theory the lowest possible temperature is $-273.15°C$. This is known as absolute zero.

zip fastener
The first successful use of the zip fastener was not in fashionable clothes but in First World War military clothing.

zodiac
The signs of the zodiac were devised in Mesopotamia nearly 5,000 years ago.

zoo
At the end of 1976 there were nearly 11,000 animals living in Whipsnade and the London Zoo in Regent's Park.

zubra
This is not a zebra spelt incorrectly, as you might expect, but the name of a type of buffalo found in Poland.